From Park Bench to Park Avenue

One Man's Journey Out of Homelessness

Anthony Brown

Copyright ©2020 Anthony Brown

Published by Square Tree Publishing
www.SquareTreePublishing.com

ISBN - 978-1-7329587-4-6

All Rights Reserved.

This book is protected by the copyright laws of the United States of America. No part of this publication may be reproduced, stored in a retrieval system, or transmitted, in any form or by any means—electronic, mechanical, photocopying, recording, or otherwise without prior written permission from the author.

Introduction

Today

Most people dream of doing things in this world. Some may aspire to be high-ranking members of society while others may settle for just having food on their table for a day. This book is about such a dream. Expansive in the way that dreams are, through these pages a journey is shared with its destination unknown. I proceeded with this project with an intended purpose, to tell a story about how one light made a difference. A light in the form of some sort of guided traveler, a person, a thing, or entity who is just like you and yet vastly different. A light that was cast into its place to shine. A light that will leave just as mysteriously as it had arrived.

On this morning of August 3, 2019, I wake up as usual; my two alarms set, one timed to go off thirty minutes after the next. After hitting the snooze button on both several times (this is something that I discovered has the most effect in getting me up on time), I wake up and roll down onto my knees for a quick prayer. These days I feel that it is important to appreciate being alive. Immediately after I pray, I start a quick review of the things that I am grateful for at this moment—how grateful I am for being alive, grateful to have a roof over my head, grateful for having a blanket to keep me warm, and my list goes on, but I must get off my knees and get ready for life.

Today is a special day for me (well, every day is

special), but this one is especially sweet—it is the opening ceremony for the school.

As I sit in the large auditorium filled with people, an image of myself is cast upon the screen behind the stage. A slight embarrassment comes over me, but I smile—I am honored to see it. I am surrounded by teachers, doctors, and professors who are now my peers. All who are new to the staff are asked to stand and as we do, we receive an enthusiastic round of applause. A yellow carnation is handed to me and many congratulations are given about. Outwardly, I smile and accept multiple handshakes when all the while inside I can't help but think, I am now a teacher.

Like everyone on this planet, I feel happy and sad; I get embarrassed and overwhelmed at times. But I am also grateful. When I think about what I have been through and what my life is like now, I am amazed at the journey that God has allowed me to take. The good times, the bad times, and even the times which I can barely remember, all seemed to have brought me here to do what is in front of me now. Either everything is a fluke, or nothing happens in God's world by mistake. I tend to think the latter, to be honest. As I sit here today reading what I've written, examining my life, I am convinced that this is what it is supposed to be at this moment. Everything has some universal order, whether it is doing laundry while the football game is on tv in the background, being stranded at the airport, frustrated as you watch your flight get cancelled again, or having a fun night out with friends, losing money playing poker with reckless abandon. It seems that no matter how you slice it, things happen, and they happen for a reason.

Just the thought that 21 years ago I was considered homeless and hopeless! I had no address, no place to call my own, no keys to anything. I had no car, no job, no education per se. It seems like a long time ago, a distant past that I am reminded of by the present realities that I witness out in this world. Today, I am becoming accepted into a position with which I can make a difference in someone else's life. I guess I am meant to be here today.

The Purpose of this Book

In the early part of 2005, my wife and I moved out of the recovery home that we oversaw, and we bought a house in California. Well, it's more like a condo but nevertheless, it is my home. When I first moved in, I would look at this place; the walls were painted yellow and the carpet was a green shag. Popcorn stucco hung to the ceiling and the place looked run down, sort of like how my life was. But little did I know that this was to become my symbol of measurement towards my spiritual awakening.

Six years prior to getting this house, I was released from yet another locked facility, as I shall describe in these pages. My only possessions were a bunch of letters that fit into a shoebox and less than $200.00 dollars in my pocket that they had given me upon my exit from Chino Correctional Facility. Once again, I had to be physically removed from society because of my out-of-control behavior.

It seems like a different life now (almost a dream at times, a different life, a different person, a different reality). It's a far cry from being housed to owning a house. From living rent free with no key, to having keys and paying monthly mortgages. From being transported, shackled to another prisoner, to having my license and driving my own car. From eating "spreads" made from Top Ramen noodles, to tipping a waitress at a restaurant. Yeah, things were once starkly different.

There are several reasons why I decided to finally sit down and write this book. First, I'm not rich. In fact, I live on a skimpy budget, but I do have Cadillac dreams. Some may call me grandiose while others have stated that I'm delusional. But nevertheless, I once heard that, "a thought without action, is only a dream," so action was needed to turn my dream into a reality. Action that took a tremendous amount of hard work, sacrifice of time, and a purposeful belief that things would be okay.

Some of the proceeds from this book will be used to renovate a historic home in Mansfield, Ohio, (see photo on the back of book) which we refer to as Brown Manor. This will be a place where individuals can go to get a fresh start, a new beginning, so to speak. A place where a new journey could start just as mine had. A steppingstone towards a new life; an oasis to come to when the journey gets weary and people are tired. I want to offer a safe place for those who are addicted to drugs or alcohol, as well as those who have mental, emotional, and psychological issues.

Brown Manor reminds me of some of the buildings that once sheltered me when I was young and homeless in that far, far away place in time that seems like a distant dream now. When I was fifteen years old, I ran away from home. I remember some of those cold dark hungry Ohio nights, huddled in a fetal position trying to stay warm, shaking not only from the outer elements of nature but also the inner pains from the hole that was developing in my soul. It was that soul sickness that I couldn't escape for many years to come.

After a meeting with some financial advisors and given the current situation of my assets, I cannot afford to build this dream on my own. So, with this book, we can all be part of something bigger than ourselves. No puzzle is completed without the individual pieces, or as the seventeenth century poet John Donne stated, "No man is an island unto himself," and this book shall be the proverbial land that connects all of us from beneath the sea.

I have reached out to several people for assistance in dealing with the crisis of addiction and mental illness, and to offer aide to the hopelessness of the homeless that we see with our eyes. It's hard to deny that there are people living in poverty because of this disease. Most freeway off-ramps in Los Angeles have a person standing by the roadside with a sign that says something to the effect of, "just feed me please." But I know from experience, in simple translation, what I hear is the message, "I have a disease, I'm dying, please hear me."

Talk is cheap from those who drive by and see this population and turn to their passenger seat and say, "Why don't they just get some help?" Wanting to help are only wishes for those who just walk past and only witness the people who are disheveled, dirty, desperate, and different. The man who is passed out in the daytime because he had nowhere to sleep the night before, now he rests in front of a restaurant with mucus streaming from his nose, while others, sharply dressed, return from church to enjoy brunch. Or the woman with the matted bun on top of her head, who at one point took pride with her long flowing hair, is unable to comb it due to the reality that the psychotropic medications that she was prescribed weren't individualized enough to resolve her neurochemical imbalance.

I can relate to both sides of the proverbial coin, and I want to make a difference. However, I don't think standing by the freeway with a truthful sign that states, "I want to renovate a house," would bring in much money. Besides, I think that is illegal.

Perhaps the response would be minute, so I figured that I would generate the revenue for this project by writing this book. So those of you who are reading this can honestly say that you have contributed by assisting in dealing with the crisis of homelessness with its elements of substance abuse and mental illness. Being aware is half the battle. Having the ability to do something is another.

One of the reasons as to why I picked Ohio was because I was born there and that is where my brother resides. Currently he is a victim to the disease of drug abuse, and it is hard for me to know that I could do something and yet not do it. There are also other people who, too, are suffering, whose names I do not yet know, who could benefit from having treatment in their neighborhood. This is a way that I could help them find the light. The same light that I have discovered on my journey. The journey in which all of you will take with me, once again, through these pages.

Still another reason for sharing my path is for the many people who have watched my journey, asking me for years to tell my story to the world. I was reluctant to do so because of my fear of society's stigma towards addiction, and that once this door is opened, others in my outside world may close. But there comes a time when fear be damned, and faith is my strength. I have worked my way up from the Park Bench to literally moving to Park Avenue and thereby, becoming a respected member of society. I didn't want to expose myself to the unnecessary fear from those who are close minded. However, I am now driven by what I see every day; whether it's on the news or in my face, I feel the need to do something that is greater than myself.

The final reason why I'm writing this book is that I have insomnia, and this is one way that I can deal with that instead of just lying in bed watching time tick by.

Table of Contents

Chapter One	Why am I Here?	1
Chapter Two	Back to the Ville	15
Chapter Three	I Went to a Party	25
Chapter Four	Running From Myself	37
Chapter Five	California Dream	45
Chapter Six	Insane Addict	53
Chapter Seven	New Beginning	73
Chapter Eight	Slip & Skirt	91
Chapter Nine	Road of Happy Destiny	101
Chapter Ten	Education is the Key	113
Chapter Eleven	Spiritual Awakening	127
Chapter Twelve	Park Bench	137

Chapter One
Why am I Here?

She screamed and cursed out loud into the silent space, and I felt helpless to do anything about it. The nurses and doctors in the operating room only did their job. The blood squirted upwards at the first incision, then sprayed across her abdomen and dripped into a plastic bag that surrounded the lower portion of her stomach. I heard someone command in an anxious voice, "Hurry, the umbilical cord is strangling him." The blood was thin, diluted from the gin that she was always known to consume, as they continued the c-section. She cursed again as her uterus was ripped open, and the premature baby was pulled from her. He was blue, incased in some substance thickened with blood. The cord was cut from around the neck, and it felt painful. The infant cried, but no sound came from it. The little mouth was open but filled with sand. It struggled to make a noise, and only when the substance was suctioned from its mouth, there was a cold ear-piercing noise.

I awoke from that dream, startled, scared, and lost again. It felt so real, and yet it was just another nightmare that I had from time to time. I looked around my bedroom, and as my eyes slowly adjusted to the darkness, I felt a tear drop from them. My thoughts raced once again, in overdrive as usual, this impatient committee inside my head waiting for me to return from slumber, anxious to remind me that I am still me, and it's time to face the day.

Ever wake up somewhere in life and wonder, "Why am I here?" That is a question that I ponder quite often, seeking the answer or at least trying to find a way to justify the reason things happen. I think, "Ah, I finally got the answer," only to feel I have no real control. My quest pushes the answers farther from me, and they become more Illusive than ever.

When I have worn out the snooze button on both my alarm clocks and finally sit up in bed, I look out into reality and ask myself, "Why am I here?" Then I roll out of my bed and fall directly to my knees to begin my morning prayers, and ask myself again, "Why am I here?" Prayers are the best way for me to start the day, normally quieting my thoughts, but on this morning, I think maybe I should have stayed on my knees longer because my 'committee' was loud and more persistent than usual.

As I stumble to the bathroom to relieve my bladder

Why am I Here?

of its contents from the night before, I ponder the same question, "Why am I here?" I wonder what the response would be from my bladder if it could ask the question, "Why am I here?" What would my commode say to this question? What about the basin in the sink? What about the spigot that produces the water? What about the cloth that I wash my face with? The soap, the toothbrush, the toothpaste, my teeth, my mouth, my eyes?

What is the true answer to this question? What would everyone else think if they were to ask themselves this question with complete sincerity? What would the answer be from the leaders of nations, news commentators, and baristas at coffee shops? What about famous people like Oprah Winfrey, Dr. Phil, Spike Lee? What would they answer to this question? What about those who stand at the altar engaging in the union, pledging rights and obligations to one another, to make that commitment of forever matrimony? I wonder if that event warrants the question of, "Why am I here?" What about divorce? Why am I here, giving birth to a child and the pains of labor when you're passing an eight-pound human? Why am I here standing at a funeral in the rain? Why am I here in this office sorting through paperwork? Why am I here looking at this mountain of bills? Why am I here, homeless, eating out of a trash can? Why am I here at the barstool drinking again? Why am I here sitting on the curb with flashing lights above me? Why am I here in this meeting saying that I am an alcoholic and my life is unmanageable? Why am I here with you? Why am I here in front of you? Why am I here behind you? Why am I here beside you? Why am I here without you?

The answer to this question is enormous and is required. However, once this ball gets rolling, who knows where it would stop? One could say that death would be a final answer, but then when you stand before the Almighty, the question still could apply. "Hey God, why am I here?"

The committee is quiet now, and I can move on to the business of linear thinking.

For years people have been asking me to write a book–tell my story, to let the world know what happened once I personally asked that same question—and to give details to the answers that I have received. The life that I was given, the experiences that I've encountered and some of the events that transpired.

For years I have contemplated this request, but as with any thought I eventually let it fade into the dark recesses of my mind. Life gets busy, and I am off to the next job, task, or whatever project that falls into my path. But finally, I have heard this request long enough and decided to do it; to pen my memoir so the world can see. Expose my truths on paper just as I have verbally stated the short version so many times to remain sane. Literally, I am putting my life into your hands.

Beginnings

It had to be around December of 1960, when my 23-year-old mother, who already had a six-year-old son and a three-month-old daughter, conceived me. When I think about the actual growth and development of life—the formation of a human being—I find it fascinating; cells multiplying and dividing, tissue and organs growing, systems being created. I wonder if each cell were to ask that question, "Why am I here?" The answer could have been something like, "To chill out and develop for about nine months because it's cold outside." After nine months of hanging about, many conversations took place. They chatted about becoming the shape of a male and about having black curly hair. They talked about the color, size and depth of the brown eyes they would create. They discussed hands, feet, lips, and all sorts of things. It must've seemed like one joyous party was going on, as the cells continued growing by the minute! They were uniting and dividing, moving and grooving, and shaping and shifting while outwardly my mother was showing and growing. However, the one thing that the ovum never discussed throughout this entire process was that wrapped inside, somewhere in her DNA, there was a defect on chromosome 15, particularly gene GABRG3.

This man whose DNA I was to inherit was named Robert. A man with whom I would have no real connection or relationship to whatsoever.

In a small town that sits along the Ohio River, called Steubenville, my mother and older brother and sister awaited my arrival. In September of 1961, I was born to join them. If I was to apply my question of "why am I here" at that time, my answer would have been, "To create sibling rivalry."

My sister was now no longer the youngest and I needed the attention. Two years later, my mother gave birth to my younger sister, and that is my family.

Rumors were, at the time, that my mother craved sand throughout her pregnancy with me, and I was born surrounded in it. From what I understand, having PICA during pregnancy is not uncommon (here I thought I was special). If the sand that she was consuming at this point would've asked, "Why am I here?", the answer would probably be, "To supply the mineral iron." To complicate matters further, it was also said that my umbilical cord was wrapped around my neck twice, and I was suffocating and blue (again, not uncommon). Apparently, since I am writing this book I survived—meaning that I was born to have this journey.

My mother drank a lot of alcohol and it was probably because she inherited my grandparents' gene GABRG3, but nevertheless, there were four of us children to look after. My brother didn't have to ask, "Why am I here?" because it was obvious, he was the babysitter.

Robert, who is my father, I have never met; his name is only known to me because it is written on my birth certificate. He may have asked himself that question, "Why am I here?" too, back then. Perhaps his answer might have been, "I am married to another woman and this will only get me into trouble, so I'd better get the hell out of Dodge." Maybe that is why I have never met him. However, my brother and sisters have met their fathers. Neither one of us have the same father, but that's okay, my mother sufficed as the glue that held us together.

Before my youngest sister was born, Mom moved us out of Steubenville and into Cleveland, Ohio. I was around the age of 18 months when this occurred, and if you were to ask me, "Why am I here?" at this point, my answer would have been, "I'm an infant and have no other choice." I remember that we moved around quite a bit in those days. Once in Cleveland, we lived above a bar. When I was eight years old, I was standing on the roof of the bar that doubled as the yard of our house. If we had a dog at that time who dug holes, it would have literally tunneled through the ceiling of the bar! I still remember that day, looking over into the alley down below and seeing a man shot and killed in front of me.

Early Memories

As far as I can remember, my mother was a daily drinker, and so were the acquaintances that she had kept throughout her life. I had many 'uncles', even though she was an only child; they all drank and would fight each other on many occasions. The one that stands out in my mind more than any other was George. George was married, but he would visit my mother throughout the week then go home to his wife on the weekends. Both my mother and George would buy different bottles of liquor and then the drinking would commence. Shortly thereafter, the verbal assaults would take place between them, which would eventually lead up to physical aggression. Day in and day out this cycle would continue, and when the weekend came and he left, Mom would be there drinking with only us to argue and fight with.

I cannot remember when my grandparents were married to each other, but I can remember my grandmother and grandfather when they were married to other people. My grandmother Hazel was nice, to a certain degree, and my grandfather John, as far as I could remember, used to give us gifts when we were younger.

The school that I attended from preschool to grade six was Charles H. Lake Elementary school. I remember walking to school. In the wintertime it snows quite a bit back east, so I'd pull these big rubber boots with buckles on the front over my tennis shoes. My coat was warm and buttoned to the top, barely allowing me to breath with my scarf wrapped around my neck and mouth. My Mom would often walk with me to school on those snowy days. I remember that I had my mittens safety pinned to the inside of my sleeves because I would always lose them. If my boots and mittens would have asked, "Why am I here?" I bet they would say, "to keep you from getting frost bite." Once at school, I had to unravel myself from the little cocoon Mom had bundled me in, in order to participate in activities in class.

That's where I learned the most important things that one can at such a young age. I sampled many jars of LePage's school paste, which was chunky and had a minty flavor. I had my wooden ruler, my weird shaped Pink Pearl eraser, and my box of Crayola crayons (which were tasty, too). It's funny, the things you remember most.

Then once school was over, I had to rewrap myself for my journey home. When I got home, I'd place the mittens on the steam radiator to dry. I can recall my favorite lunch box—the one with Snoopy from Peanuts on it—and the thermos that had hot chocolate in it or that sometimes held a surprise of warm Cream of Wheat cereal.

Thermos' back then were made quite differently, and I was told firmly by Mom not try to clean it, but only to rinse it out. One day I decided to take it apart to see what that silver thing was inside the plastic. I discovered it was made of glass and once I unscrewed the bottom, it fell out and broke. I cleaned up the glass, screwed the thermos back together and placed it back into my lunchbox. Well, the next day when Mom went to fill up my thermos with hot chocolate, it all seeped out from the bottom and I was busted. Now I know why I shouldn't have tried to clean it.

Ohio, Christmas and Dysfunction

Thinking about Ohio winters makes me nostalgic of the simple days in life. Looking out the window, seeing the snow start to fall, drawing faces on the glass in the condensation. I feel a warmth of happiness in these thoughts. When I think hard enough, I can recall some of the scents from the food Mom used to cook. Homemade macaroni and cheese, corn bread, meatloaf, greens. I remember she used to make three cakes at the same time because my sisters and I all have our birthdays within a twenty-day time frame. I smile when I remember just waiting for Mom to finish mixing the cake so that I could get the remaining batter from the bowl. I'd scrape my fingers around the edges, then lick them clean.

I also remember Christmas at that time. The silver Evergleam stainless aluminum two-foot Christmas tree that came in the white box and had a Christmas ribbon painted on it. We would pull out each branch from the sleeves and insert them into the holes that we predrilled on the pole that was the base. The ornaments were green, blue, and red bulbs that we hung with care because the price for breaking a bulb was costly. The different colors of the tree reflected the colors of red, green, blue, and amber from the rotating wheel that sat in the corner. Christmas was fun, with toys, fruits, nuts, and in the family punchbowl was the best part of this holiday… eggnog with rum! Oh, how I loved Christmas time! But after the punchbowl was emptied, fights would eventually happen, sometimes knocking the tree over. Once we found toys hidden under the bed, and Santa had been exposed! After that, he didn't come down our chimney as often. However, the punchbowl always presented its greetings so who cared about Saint Nick when you had eggnog laced with rum?

I also remember Mom would get so drunk she could barely move from the couch. She would command me and my sisters to cook her scrambled eggs. She used to say that I could make them the best. The trick was to make them just right. She would want them slightly "runny" but not overcooked. However, if I missed the mark and the eggs weren't "just right," I would get a plate full of eggs thrown at me. I wasn't very quick back then, so I know what it's like to get hit with a dish of hot food. Cooking is something, that to this day, I still don't like doing.

Saying that I had a good childhood is a stretch of the imagination. The title of dysfunctional would be a proper label if I were to place one on it. My mother worked all day, as most single parents do these days, and at night she would come home and make sure we were all fed. But being raised with her being gone most of the time meant we were alone quite a bit. When she wasn't there, we kids did as kids do.

Whoopings

We moved once again. This time our house had wooden floors. I remember this because my sisters and I would entertain ourselves by dragging each other across the hardwood floors with a blanket. I remember once getting a splinter in my foot and crying to Mom only to receive a whooping for getting injured. As you can see, my mother believed in the, "Spare the rod and spoil the child," theory, so whoopings were served plentiful. During that time period, my brother thought that this was a good opportunity to leave and my grandmother took him in. He was fifteen at that time, and that was the last time that I saw him in Cleveland. I was about seven years old.

Other than playing house games with my two sisters, we discovered where Mom's gin was kept. She hid it under the kitchen sink. When she went to work, we found that drinking the gin would make things a lot more fun. The more that we drank when Mom wasn't home, the more reckless we became in the house. The more reckless we were in the house, the more Mom would drink. The more that Mom would drink, the more whoopings we received. Back in those days, there was a man in Mom's life who my sisters and I called Dad. Dad drank just as much as Mom, and then both of them would get drunk and we would receive whoopings twofold. That was how it went in those days.

I looked forward to going to school because at least that got me out of the house. Back then, however, the teachers were allowed to give you swats and I got my fair share of them. I understand now that I was acting out for a reason. I was always trying to get attention; I talked back to the teachers and got plenty of swats from everyone. I remember that one of the punishments that I received from school was that I had to stand up in class and hold a number of dictionaries straight-out from my body and if I dropped them, I would receive a swat. I think the most that I had to hold was six at one time.

Either way, I was going to get a beating from someplace, so why even try to do anything, right? The more whoopings I got at home, the more swats I got at school, so I continued to act out all the more. I started mouthing off to anyone that I wanted to; I got into fights with anyone that I wanted to—at that point in time I was a ten-year-old who really didn't care about anything. That was until the day when my sisters and I suddenly woke up in the middle of the night to find my mother lying on the floor in the living room surrounded by a puddle of blood. She had been shot in the head. The bullet went into the center of her forehead and exited behind her left ear. Dad had disappeared, and the world seemed a blank after that.

Chapter Two
Back to the Ville

Seeing someone up close with a gunshot wound to the head is a sight for anyone—let alone a ten-year-old child. Maybe you hear about something like this happening when kids are out playing in the woods or trespassing in an abandoned house. As for me at the age of ten, I am suddenly forced to carry the memory of a woman lying on the cold hard wooden living room floor with blood slowly pooling underneath her head. I cannot remember the position of her body, but I can remember the blood and chunks of gray matter that were there and me calling, "Mom, Mom…" and her not moving at all. Calling her name over and over until the tears blocked my vision. That thought—seared into my brain—still has the same effect on me today as it did back then. The image of the hole in the center of her forehead, and how it was revealed to me that the exit point was behind her ear—I can never erase from my mind.

Moving Again

Miraculously, Mom had survived her injuries, but she wore bandages around her head for some time. We moved back to Steubenville. We moved into an apartment on South Eighth Street, and all we brought with us was one suitcase and the three coats that my sisters and I were wearing. It was all that we owned then. It was so cold in those days, and we were hungry. I smile thinking of one of the first meals that we enjoyed: spaghetti with butter on it! We couldn't afford sauce, and the dish that we ate out of was an empty Vienna sausage can. We had no furniture, but that was fine, because we had Mom. She had lived and whatever happened to Dad, we didn't know. However, through all of this, Mom had changed.

Steubenville, Ohio, is a city located in Jefferson County, Ohio, United States. It derives its name from Fort Steuben, a 1786 fort that sat within the city's current limits and was named for German-Prussian military officer, Baron Friedrich Wilhelm von Steuben. We natives call it "The Ville", and for me, it was and always will be called home. The Ville was a small town that was full of action. There were places to go to get booze at night (after hours joints), there was a whore house, and bars—all controlled by individuals who were part of the Mafia. It is the birthplace of singer and actor Dean Martin, actress Traci Lords, television commentator and odds maker Jimmy "The Greek" Snyder, and Hall of Fame baseball pitcher, Rollie Fingers.

When I think about the Ville, I remember the five and dime stores like McCrory's and Kresge's. I remember fountain drinks and penny candy. I remember the Hub which was a big department store, the Grand Theater, and The Jefferson County Courthouse and the police station that was behind it. I remember the Market Street Bridge which connected on the other side to West Virginia and Route 2 in Follansbee, over the Ohio River.

I close my eyes and can remember Naples Spaghetti House, chipped chopped ham from Islay's Restaurant, the Harold Star Newspaper Company, and George's Coffee Shop with the pool hall next to it. There was Saint Paul's Church (where Granny worked), Myer and Stones Men's Wear, Denmark's and the First National Bank. I can still remember the glass bottles of milk from Spahn's Dairy. Great memories from a time once long gone. It seems odd that I had suppressed all those thoughts until now.

My grandmother (Granny) was also from "The Ville", and I remember that she and my mother used to argue all the time. My brother was living with Gran at the time, up the hill on Parkview Circle, and I cannot recall them ever coming to our house, but what I do remember is having to go to school there in the six grade. And all the while Mom continued to drink.

If the Adverse Childhood Experience (ACE's)[1] were given in my household, I would have scored an eight by now. This is a test that asks if you have experienced household dysfunction, abuse, or neglect before the age of eighteen. I was high up on the scale, and I was just turning ten. According to the results of the ACE's study, if you scored four or more, you're likely to have problems with alcoholism as an adult; if you scored six or more, you're likely to be a smoker; if you scored four or more, you are likely to have poor work performance. Plus, the higher the score, the more likely you are to have emotional problems. I had passed that threshold and still had eight more years to go!

Life Back Then

I attended Grant Jr. High that was located on South Fourth Street. I was the new kid on the block, and since we had moved during the middle of the school year, I had the pleasure of finishing the sixth grade making new friends. I remember all the fights that I got into, so school sucked big time. I did what I knew to do, which was acting out, so I got swats at school once again, went home with Mom drinking and got whoopings there. When Mom wasn't looking, I got

---

[1] The Adverse Childhood Experiences Study (ACE Study) is a research study conducted by the U.S. health maintenance organization Kaiser Permanente and the Centers for Disease Control and Prevention.[1] Participants were recruited to the study between 1995 and 1997 and have been in long-term follow up for health outcomes. The study has demonstrated an association of adverse childhood experiences (ACEs) (aka childhood trauma) with health and social problems across the lifespan. The study has produced many scientific articles and conference and workshop presentations that examine ACEs.

into her gin, got drunk and eventually fell asleep. I didn't know this at the time, but my life was being shaped into what I would spend years trying to escape from. I made it from the sixth grade, moving upstairs to the seventh and Jr. High. I was twelve years old, and Mom had gotten a job working as a janitor. She had saved up enough money for us to move from the South End of the Ville to the North End of town.

I remembered the house on Ross Street because this was the first and only house that I can recall that Mom had owned. It was a two-story house with a wooden porch swing. We used to sit on it and look across the street and see the empty lot that stood next to the Brown's house. I remember the twins, Karen and Sharon, and their younger sister, Brenda, and how we played with them often. Up the street and across the alley was where my cousin, Tim, his brother, Shawn, and my aunt, Juju, lived. Even though my mother was the only child, we had aunts.

Across North Fifth Street was The Keg liquor store. The owners were John and Pat. I was with John the day he found Pat cheating on him, and he beat the crap out of the guy right there in front of me. Further east down the street past Fifth Street was Brian's house. Brian was cool because he had a pool table in his place, and I could go down there and play pool quite often. Jamie lived on Six Street and Jimmy, on Fifth, close to Logan Avenue. The projects were further north next to the ball field, and then there was the underpass that led you up hill to Winterville. That is basically the North End of Steubenville.

Hidden Gin

As you walked through the front door of our Ross Street house, there was a foyer and then to the left, a staircase that led upstairs. Directly in front of the entrance was a closet (which one day my younger sister and I were playing and fell into the closet wall and damaged the plasterboard. We covered the hole up with wallpaper so Mom wouldn't find out). As you walked on past, you came to the T.V. room. On the opposite side of the foyer was the living room. It was decked out in gold carpet and the sofa and love seat were covered in plastic. The lamps were the same color as the carpet and Mom still kept the plastic from the factory on the lampshades. The living room was definitely off limits to the kids. Walking straight as you exited the living room, you entered the dining room. There was a table with eight chairs and a hutch where the fine china was stored. Past the dining room was the kitchen and it was here that Mom hid her gin under the sink.

In towns such as The Ville, we had four seasons, and thinking about this house, what I remembered the most was fall. Ohio is known as the Buckeye State and there was plenty of buckeyes laying around. We used to use them to launch out of the slingshots that we would make out of wire coat hangers, rubber bands, and a patch of cloth. I smile when I think about the autumn days when the leaves would turn brown and fall to the ground. Then I would rake them up in a pile and jump into them, just to have to rake them up again.

Making Friends and Skipping School

The South End of The Ville had streets like Linden Ave., Spring, Railroad, South Street, Hill Ave, and the South End projects. The North End had streets like Logan Ave., Superior, Ross, Madison, Franklin, Sherman, and the North End projects. The separation was Market Street. Up the Hill was Wintersville, and across the Ohio River was West Virginia.

Jamie (from Sixth Street) and I were friends then, and he had an older sister named Tess who I secretly had a crush on. We started hanging around, smoking cigarettes and sipping beer. We'd get drunk, skip school and hang out downtown. We used to go bumper skiing a lot (when a car stops at the stop sign during the winter and there's snow on the ground, you grab the bumper and hang on). We'd ride trains (run along the side of a moving train and jump on the ladders). Jamie and I were like two peas in a pod.

During the seventh grade I met a new friend named Mark, who was an outcast like I was, and we hit it off pretty well. He lived past the South End, down Sinclair Ave. Mark would come to school with cigarettes rolled up in his shirt and cuss like a true seventh grader. Mark and I would then skip school and hang out at his house. Then I met Artie, Lori, Bill, and Tom. I had found a home and friends.

Tom and Bill were older than the rest of us, they had cars, and they could buy beer. When I would walk from my house on the North End all the way to Sinclair Ave, I had to pass Grant Jr. High school. As long as I got home in time, that was okay, but it really didn't matter because the whoopings were plenty, and I had plenty of years for that. But none of that mattered at the time, because I had friends and I was accepted.

In the winter, of course, it snowed, but that did not keep me from finding some way to skip school and head over to Mark's. There was more than one occasion when Mark's father was home and we'd still skip school. We just hid out across the street from the school, inside an abandoned building, and drank from the little bottle of gin that I had stolen from Mom's stash that was hidden under the kitchen sink. Hiding across from the school didn't always pan out that well, for the truant officer would see us and we'd run. More than once we'd get caught and were forced to go back into school. On those occasions we were greeted with the paddle. It really didn't matter much to me, I was used to that by then. I recall one day when the principal called Mom and reported my antics. Mom came down to the school, took me into the book room that was next to the principal's office on the third floor and beat me with an extension cord. I think that the embarrassment of my yelling and screaming that echoed down the hall during class created more lasting pain than the actual beating. But I took it, and finished class, walked home and was greeted with yet another unpleasant welcome.

Back to the Ville

That year I had to repeat the seventh grade, and my life was pretty much set as to my teen years. I continued to miss school, getting drunk as much as I could, and receiving the beatings that came with it. At that time, Mom decided to buy our first—and only house—on Ross Street, and she continued to work her way up in life. She was going to school and eventually became a nurse. I can still see her in her white uniform, the white shoes and stockings and the black strip she used to sport on her cap. We all moved in and my two sisters and I thought things were looking up for our single parent family. At least cosmetically.

During that period of time, my younger sister and I had started to sneak Mom's cigarettes, but of course I couldn't tell her that I was already a pro at smoking. My younger sister had a habit of always telling Mom the things that I would do even though she was always ready to get involved in my shenanigans. My older sister was more of an authoritarian and quite bossy. She was really like Mom and would beat me up as well. So, there I was, the boy in the middle of two girls. On more than one occasion my younger sister would do something to piss me off, and then my older sister would beat me up. Then they would both tell Mom, and I'd get another beating when she came home.

There was one time in which we were sitting up inside a window on the second floor of our house, and we would act like we were going to push each other out of the window but at the last minute, we'd grab each other's waist to prevent us from actually falling out. One day during this game, I

From Park Bench to Park Avenue

forgot to grab my cousin Brenda's waist, and she went flying out of the second story window. She broke her arm and guess what happened when Mom came home?

Thank God for marijuana.

Chapter Three
I Went to a Party

Alcohol and drug addiction come with numerous interpretations. Some say that it is a mind, body, and spiritual disease. I have heard that in the mind, it is a mental obsession coupled with a severe compulsion to find relief from thinking. Neurons located in the brain show when dopamine is released in this area; it creates a strong reward to the brain, so once an addictive substance is introduced, the more these neurons are excited, the more reward you get, and that leads to a person wanting to consume more of the substance.[2]

The spiritual part refers to not adhering to what is right and being involved in several levels of what some would deem "sins". If I were to look at the common seven

---
2   This is known as the "phenomenon of craving".

behaviors of pride, greed, lust, envy, gluttony, wrath, and sloth and view them in excess, it creates a disconnection with Our Creator. Abuses of these seven sins puts us in conflict with mankind.

Addictions are progressive. Due to your body's tolerance, you ingest an amount, but then it takes more and more to reach the same effect over time. Once you've crossed a certain point in substance use, you tend to lose control over all aspects of your life. Things pile up and become unsolvable, and in order to deal with life, you continue this vicious cycle. Had I have known all of this then, plus the fact that I have possibly inherited the alcohol genetics (GABRG3), I might have taken a different route of action to resolve my dilemma. But that's not how my story goes…

Trying Not to Feel

I would do anything to not feel anymore. Or maybe do anything to feel something. I can't kill myself because if I'm not successful, I'll get my ass beat. I don't fit in anywhere, don't belong anywhere. I am a nobody, and nobody cares. I am nothing and nothing matters. How can I feel pain when everything I have encountered has been painful? How can a broken child that only knows brokenness, fix itself? I am so traumatized that I'm borderline delusional, and nobody seems to care that I'm crazy. I cannot escape from the prison that is me, I am trapped.

My younger sister and I had discovered that if you rolled up tea (yes, that is Lipton tea) into a zig-zag rolling paper, you could smoke it and it smells like marijuana. So, since I was well into knowing the effects of alcohol, then this feeling that I was getting from the Lipton tea was meaning that I was getting high. So, based upon my infinite wisdom, the first time that I got high was with Lipton tea. Now, based upon my current knowledge, I know that it's biochemically impossible for tea to give you the same effects of marijuana. However, in my mind back then, I was buzzed. So, we continued to smoke tea and drank almost anything that we could get our hands on. I do recall that there was a time in which we attempted to make some homemade wine out of the grapes that were growing beside our house.

Mark had some real seedy cannabis that went by the name of Acapulco Gold. I remember that we used to chant, "No stems of seeds that we don't need—Acapulco Gold is some bomb ass weed." Now that stuff was completely different than the Lipton tea that I had tried, and the effects were phenomenal. By then, I had pretty much given up on school and spent my time hanging out with Mark, Artie, Tom, and the gang. At this time Tom had scored a job at the Grand Theater cleaning up the place, and we would go in and help him. We'd get high and go up the back stairs where they had the old dressing rooms and just have a blast. The whoopings didn't matter anymore because between the weed and booze, I really wasn't that much into reality. But the problem is that both of these habits cost money.

Pills

Somehow, they passed me to the eighth grade, and that was okay. I wasn't going to school much anyway. At least I was done with the seventh grade (by that time I had repeated seventh grade three times). In order for me to supply my habit, I started working on cutting grass in the summer and shoveling snow in the winter. That got me some money but not enough because I started to discover that there were other things that I could smoke, eat, and drink to change my reality, and they were costly. I discovered Columbia Red Bud, Chocolate Tai Stick, Hash, and pills. Most of the pills back then that I tried were uppers. Things like Dexamyl (Christmas Tress), White Cross (Cross Tops), and Biphetamine (Black Beauties). I also found that beer wasn't sufficient, so I started drinking wine.

I discovered that I could shoplift wine, and I focused a lot of attention towards that, but I couldn't steal the pills or the weed. So, I started stealing things to sell to keep up my growing habit. I remember once that I shoplifted enough pairs of tennis shoes to supply the entire football team for Grant Jr. High's eighth graders. I guess that was one way to get me into the school. My sisters were progressing in school, and I think that my brother had graduated by then, but I was spending as much time as possible on the street. By then I had my first run-in with the police and was sent to juvenile hall, but that was okay, it just gave me more time away from home.

I love my mother, and as an adult, I know that she did the best that she could with what she knew. She was a hard worker, always keeping food in the house and a roof over our heads. Even after she was shot, she still continued to do her best to provide for us. Her, 'spare the rod and spoil the child,' mentality was what she was taught, so I got a taste of that philosophy in a way few may have experienced.

Big Trouble

One day Mom had gotten a job working housekeeping for a bank. She took all three of us there to help her. We would vacuum the floor, empty the trash, and wipe desks, etc. I had acquired all types of bad habits, and of course, I would exercise them wherever I was. So, during the time of cleaning the bank, I would look into the drawers of the desk and steal things like loose change, gum, and whatever I thought would have value.

During this this time of me searching for things to steal, I came across a drawer that had several brown envelopes in them. I opened them up to see the contents and to my surprise each envelope had money in it. It was the pay for the workers at the bank, and I had hit pay dirt! This was too much for me to contain, so I went and told the told the girls of my discovery. We took the money and split it up in three ways. I think the net haul was about $500.00 each. I had never seen that much money before in my life, and I was rich!!

That was the heist of the century for me. I was spending money like a millionaire. I brought my friend Jamie's Mom some White Shadow perfume from the Hub; I was buying mashed potatoes and rolls at Islays for everyone. I treated friends to meat sauce heels from Naples; pizza at DiCarlos. It was a party, and I was the Grand Marshall. I smoked and drank and lived life for as long as that $500.00 could carry a fourteen-year-old back in the seventies. Everything was wonderful…until I came home.

I walked into the door of that house at 509 Ross Street and sitting in the living room on Mom's plastic-covered couch were two Caucasian gentlemen dressed in suits and smoking cigarettes. Mom was there, and my two sisters were peeking around the room giving me the look like "it's about to go down." Before anyone could say a word, Mom asked, "Where is the money?" What was I to say? I gave the most honest answer that I could have come up with through the haze that was cooking inside my intoxicated brain. I replied, "What money?"

Mom didn't believe in holding anything back—ever. She didn't care who was there and once she unleashed the can of whoopass, the best anyone could do was to stay out of range. Before I knew it the taste of blood was in my mouth, and I was lying on the floor. The gentlemen on the plastic-covered couch smoking their cigarettes were federal agents investigating the theft. I think I heard her ask me again about the money, and before I could come up with another good lie to tell, my younger sister yelled from her corner, "Mom, he took the money and gave it to us".

Okay, now the feds got involved because when I split the money, my older sister was supposed to take the envelopes and put them into the incinerator at the bank to get rid of the evidence. But what she actually did was put the envelopes in the box *beside* the incinerator to be burned. When the bank discovered that the payroll money was missing, since it was a bank, the feds were contacted. During their investigation, they found the envelopes in the trash and started looking at the housekeeper. My Mom was the cleaning lady for the bank, so they came to our house and put the squeeze on my sisters. They both ratted me out. They still had their money and gave it back, but I had spent all of mine. The case was solved, and Mom had to pay back the money and lost her job. The feds left and Mom was to bring me to court on this matter. I wished that the feds would have taken me in with them.

Beyond Whoopings

All of us got it that night, but I know that mine was the worse. To this day, out of all the whoopings that I had experienced and all the drugs that I had put in my system, nothing, absolutely nothing, could take away the memory of this one. We had to wait until Mom went down the ranks. My oldest sister was first. As my youngest sister and I hid in the other room we could hear her cry. Mom's device of choice at that time was the extension cord. The first sister was quick, it seemed, maybe only six or seven whacks. One whack with the extension cord was painful. It leaves welts on the body, cuts the skin, and is painful as hell. My younger sister was next, she was always the weakest. Heck, she started crying and screaming before she even got the taste of it. She got only three or four whacks. Then it was my turn.

Mom made my lie on the carpeted floor, and she put her foot on my neck and started to hit me with the extension cord. I could not go anywhere, just spin in some old type of circle on the ground. I don't know how many whacks I got or how long it lasted, but what I do know is that she got tired. I remembered that I got up and tried to run, and she told me to never run from her, and I lay back on the floor. She sat down on the couch and smoked a cigarette, then got up and placed her foot back on my neck and started beating me again. I finally reached a point in which I couldn't take it anymore and ran out of the house.

I think it was Jamie that was babysitting in a house down the alley in which I fled. I got him to let me in, and I hid in the closet. I was scared, more scared than anything I had ever encountered, and I just wanted to escape. At least for that time being I had got away. Or at least, I thought. I remember hearing a knock on the front door and then it was quiet. Suddenly, the closet door opened, and it was Mom standing there! With extension cord in hand, I got a good beating inside the closet. I had no place to go, I was trapped and all I could do was beg.

She let me out and made me walk home. Every so often she would make me stop and she'd say things like, "Don't you run from me!" and then she would hit me. If I tried to protect my face, she would say, "Don't you put your hands up to me!" and then she would hit me. This lasted probably three quarters of a block until we got into the house. She was tired then, she fixed herself a drink and told me that I had better get all the money back or else.

There was no way that I could get that money back. I had spent it all. I asked Jamie's Mom for the perfume back to return to the store. I tried everything that I could to recoup whatever I could, but there was no way to get the money back. I had a rug burn on the side of my face the size of a baseball and a rug burn on the side of my body from the carpet. I had welts all over my face and body, and I had to go to school the next day—or at least walk in that direction. I think at that point in my life, I just didn't care about anything anymore. From that point on in my life, all I wanted to do was to just get as high as I could and never face reality again.

Avoiding Reality

I was fourteen then and mentally withdrawn from everything around me. Every chance I could, I'd run away from home. At this point, I called myself homeless because I felt like I didn't have a home. When I was there, I was invisible and tried to stay invisible. Whatever I could do to act out, I did. I shoplifted things to buy friendships. I stole booze as much as I could, and when Mom's supply got skimpy, I would replace her gin with water (I still to this day don't know how she got drunk considering her booze was watered down so much).

I hid outside the house, mostly, and whenever the truant officer would catch me, he would return me home and the scene would be status quo. I would stay out if I could, but my survival skills weren't that great. I would sleep in old houses around the corner from where I lived, and some neighbor would tell my location to either my sisters or my Mom. When I couldn't get out, I would barricade myself in my room, listen to Pink Floyd and smoke as much pot that I could to block out reality. However, when opportunity presented itself, I would leave and stay away as long as possible.

I finally discovered that the further away from the house that I could get, the less likely that I would get caught, so I started hitchhiking down route seven to route 22 and then up the mountain to route 213. I had some friends that lived up there and could get some pot, so I spent a lot of time there and would hide out in the woods after I got my stash. Ohio was cold in the winter, and my numb hands would always bring me back closer to home so I could sneak into the house when Mom was at work to get some food and warmth.

My survival skills were getting better, and little did I know that these would come in handy during my later years. I remember when I would walk across the rickety train bridge to a spot called Catfish pond. I'd fish using a piece of string, a stick, and a safety pin. That place was interesting because back then, if you were an African American, and you got caught by certain elements in West Virginia, life would cease to exist as you knew it. Come to think about it, I have some crazy memories about hitchhiking that were frightening at best.

This pattern continued until one day I came back to the house to pilfer some food and found that the family had all moved. The house on Ross street was vacant and Mom, along with my sisters, all packed up and moved into the projects. The Ville was such a small town that locating them wasn't hard. But the decision appeared to be made that I was best left on my own to fend for myself. I had truly been abandoned, and my thoughts said that they didn't really love me after all, so they left me. That statement was as far as the truth than anything that I could have conjured up. I presented myself upon the door to my Mom's new house, and things were certainly different. I didn't have a key to the house in the projects, so I was basically a stranger. But Mom let me in because technically, I was a minor and she was responsible for me.

The North End projects were interesting, and I met a lot of new friends. I remember Rich, who used to argue with me over Led Zeppelin being a better band than Kiss. Jack, who taught me sign language. I remember Bennie and Chris, the brothers who lived outside the projects. I remember those days but most important, I remember Skateland!

Skateland was the hangout back in the day. I can still see those brown skates and orange wheels, with the shoe size written on the backside of the heal. I remember kids would have their birthday parties there and they'd bring out this limbo stick that kids would skate under. The floor was made of concrete, and there was a disco ball that shined different colors on the floor while we'd skate to all of the top tunes of the day.

Drinking wine and eating Quaaludes while roller-skating was a feat all in itself. I'd have to bum money (panhandle) to get enough to get drunk and then, somehow, get into the rink. Once I got in, I would be so intoxicated that I'd eventually get into a fight that led me outside the rink. Then I'd put my skates back on and roll downhill all the way home. When I didn't get that loaded, I could skate pretty decent, and I'd roll around crashing into walls just to annoy people. Either way, I was a mess but that was my normal, so the party continued. Numerous times I would come to Mom's house a mess and just become more of a burden on that household.

Chapter Four

Running from Myself

There's a place that lies between sanity and insanity—I call it instability. It's a place where you start to discover that something isn't right, but you cannot pinpoint exactly what's wrong. Fact becomes fantasy, and reality's boundaries become blurred. Physical pain becomes less painful while emotional pain becomes a thing of the past. Once emotional pain is suppressed, anything physical becomes nonexistence. Thus is born the mindset, "If you don't expect nothing, when you don't get nothing, you don't have to feel nothing." The perfect recipe for survival.

Home was never the same for me after that day. I never wanted to be in the house, and it seemed that Mom had changed as well. She drank a little more each day. She continued going to school and was determined to give us a life, but I really didn't care if I had one.

I started hanging out at some maintenance shack that was in the alley behind Old Gill hospital. It was right across the alley from the ambulance company that shared the garage with the Checker Cab company. There was a wire hoop on the outside of the building which we would play basketball with. Inside was an old man named John. John was cool. He would let us come in during the winter, share his lunch with us, give us some tea out his old thermos and teach us how to play the board game, Parcheesi. I spent a lot of time down there in that shack; it was safe.

I remember we used to play a game where we would sit on top of the back of someone's car and when they would drive away, we would jump off once the speed got too fast. One day, I was riding on the back of John's car while eating an orange, and he must have not known that I was there and accelerated. I lost my grip, fell off the car and hit my head on the ground. I went unconscious and when I woke up, I was in the hospital. I was told that when I hit my head, I was in the process of eating an orange and that it had lodged into the back of my throat. I was lucky to be alive! Then I saw Mom in the room. She just scolded me for not having clean underwear on. (Personally, I think every fourteen-year-old wears dirty underwear).

The Navy

I think that Mom was getting tired of the "spare the rod, spoil the child" thing and decided to work on another strategy. She saw that I was going nowhere fast and officially took me out of school. Finally, she was starting to understand. Let me be me and everything would be fine. I could party freely and do whatever I wished. But Mom had other plans. Before I knew what was happening, she had me at the Armed Forces Recruiting Office and somehow enlisted me into the Navy. The Navy! So, on December 29th, 1976, just four days after Christmas and in the dead of winter, I was sent to the Great Lakes Naval Training Station in Illinois. This was not part of my plan, and I did not do well with authority. Plus, how was I going to get high in the Navy? I had to get out and get out soon.

    Somehow, I got the nick name boots and I met a guy whose name when abbreviated was S.O.X. So, we teamed up and were referred to as Boots and Sox. This was cool, but I had to get out of the Navy. So, I did what I knew to do and acted out. The Navy was a little different than acting out with Mom. They had this program in which you would stay in there and learn to act right. It was way too cold to have to march all the time, and I was not liking it one bit. However, the more that I acted out, the more I marched in the snow. I did this for six weeks. Finally, I was given an honorable discharge. I found out many years later that they didn't let me out because they gave in to my nonsense; they let me out because they had found out that I was only fifteen years old!

Running

    I continued to find ways to run, and really, all I was trying to do was to escape from myself. I just could not deal with life as it presented itself, and the thought of having to be at home was too much. So, one day while I was at a carnival in Wintersville, I decided to leave with them when they left town.

    I became a carnie and loved it. I had all the time in the world to do whatever, whenever I wanted. The carnie life for me was one big party. I got to travel around Ohio for free, and no one could tell me nothing. I had run away from home, and no one knew where I was. I was told that my Mom was looking for me, but I could hide well. No one knew how old I was, and no one really asked. It was hard work, but that was okay—a great trade-in for a lifestyle of partying. Life was going my way, and I was loving it. I remember having some drunken brawls during my first year. There was even one time in which we were in Colliers, West Virginia—I woke up one night only to discover that I was covered in shattered glass. During my sleep, someone had taken a hatchet and chopped the door up, shattering glass everywhere!

    I remember the amusement ride that I used to oversee, called The Tip Top. My job was to assemble it, operate it, then when we were done after ten days or so, disassemble it and go on to the next town. The ride itself had six tubs people would sit in and turn the wheel that was in the middle, so the entire tub would spin around. While the tub spun, the platform that it was sitting on would turn clockwise and then tilt up in the air by compressed air.

    This is where I slept at night—under this ride. If you

looked closely underneath it when the platform lifted, you could see my sleeping bag, blankets, and clothes that were hanging on the frame for drying. Sometimes people would get sick from spinning so fast and vomit inside of the tub or on the platform. We would just get a bucket of water to wash the stuff off the ride (cotton candy and corn dogs are gross when regurgitated). The water would run downward and onto my belongings. I'd use that same bucket to wash my clothes at night.

Showers in those days consisted of a garden hose attached to the metal fencing that was put up in the center of the ride to brace the light poles that supported the platform. On warm days, I had warm showers and on cold days, cold showers. We could take draws (money advancements from our pay), so we could buy food from the food trailers that were on the lot. Most of the time, I would just get credit at the food trailer and still get the draw, so I could buy drugs. My pay at the end of the week was skimpy, but that is the life I chose at that time.

I had only the clothes on my back when I joined the carnies. I wore the same thing for days, and I think someone had given me a blanket from somewhere. I would get so dirty during set up (assembly) and tear down (disassemble) because amusement rides have hydraulic oils, grease, and dirt. Plus, the lots that we'd set up in were vacant and dirty. After we'd get the ride up, I would take a shower with my clothes on and wash them at the same time. The sun would dry them when it was sunny outside. But if it was cold, I just didn't bathe or wash them. There were times when others would get arrested for one reason or another, and when that occurred, their belongings would be left behind. That is how I got my sleeping bag and other clothes.

Carnival season typically runs from April through October, and once it's over everybody goes home or gets the opportunity to stay at winter quarters. I wasn't able to go to winter quarters, so I was stuck with the fact that I had to go home and deal with Mom, who hadn't seen me in seven months. I went home, and the best I could do was to walk in the door and give her the money that I had from my bonus. Mom, to my surprise, was happy to see that I was alive and welcomed me home. Me, on my part, I had been drinking and using drugs for so long, I couldn't stop the madness, even if I wanted to. It wasn't long until one day, Mom came into my bedroom and found me laying in my bed on my back covered in vomit. I remember laying there watching the ceiling spin and couldn't even move. I just threw up in the air, and it came back down on me. Mom dragged me off, put me in the bathtub and told me that she could not live like this anymore.

She was right, and maybe she wasn't the one with the problem. Maybe I might have had some part in all of the chaos. After all, I always wanted to get away, anyhow, so I moved out of her house and into an abandoned house in the Ville. This was okay, but I had nothing except for a bad habit that seemed to be in control of my life. So, I found some wooden crates that doubled as furniture, and set up my domicile.

Homeless

The winter months of Ohio are cold, and with no utilities in my new dwellings, I had to burn my furniture in the fireplace to keep warm. The only problem with this was that once smoke went out of the chimney, the police saw it and came to evict me out of the abandoned dwelling. This went on for years—in the summer I was a carnie, and in the winter I was homeless. But I didn't have a problem. I wanted to party and that I got to do. By then, I was into almost anything that I could put into my body. It didn't matter how it got inside me, as long as I thought that it worked, I did it. I was at the point that if someone would have told me to put sand in my butt, I would go find a beach and do a naked booty scoot!

I once squatted in a place that was across from Skateland. Somehow the utilities were still on, so that made it a nice place to live and party in. I had accumulated furniture from places (real furniture, not the typical wooden crates) and had made this my home. It turned into a party house, and I lived the high life. During this period of my life, I must admit that the only skills I had were raking leaves, shoveling snow, selling drugs and stealing. So, when there weren't leaves or snow or I had no drugs to sell (hard to keep a supply when I kept sampling), I was left to one skill. One day I got the idea that I needed a refrigerator and that there was one in the empty house next to mine. How did I know that that this house was empty? Well, I just knew. So, I decided to take it, but when I was pulling it up the hill, some guy saw me, and I was caught in the act. He beat me up pretty good and I called the police on him. That was my best thinking, but when the cops came, they sided with him and allowed him to take the fridge back. On top of that, he was never charged for the assault, and the police kicked me out of my squatted domicile.

Life in the Ville was not working for me. I couldn't find a steady job, had no place to live and most of my friends were not being friendly. No one seemed to want a homeless drug addict coming over to mooch for a Christmas meal. Mom's door was always open, but she had gotten to the point where I was not allowed to just walk in and raid the refrigerator. She said that I could eat, but it seemed that I couldn't have all that I wanted to consume. I had burnt that bridge to the ground. But just as my luck had it, my friend Jimmy had just come back from California. He said that he had relatives out there. I agreed eagerly to go and off we went.

Chapter Five
California Dream

Doing a geographical change in my location wasn't really a choice. Hell, what difference did it make anyway? If I could get three thousand miles away from home, maybe I could do something different. The problem is that I was taking **me** with me. The problem wasn't the environment that I was in, it was the environment that I created around me. I was the living dead, held together with booze and drugs. The brown eyes that sat in my head were lifeless, a reminder of the soul that they connected to.

I learned how to drive a car cruising down interstate seventy for three days with my friend, Jimmy, and his dog, Rocky. Up until that point, I was eighteen years old and had never driven a car. We were in a sixty-seven Mustang, and everything that I owned was in an old army duffle bag in the back seat that Rocky threw up on several times. All that I knew about California was that there were palm trees, beaches, and the Beverly Hillbilly Show. I thought that everyone lived a glamorous lifestyle, and Jimmy had me sold on living the dream.

This adventure should have been easy. Jimmy had relatives out here that he knew, and I knew Jimmy. At least I knew him from back home. What's interesting about our relationship was that we used to be enemies. But now that we were headed to California, a strange environment with people that I didn't know, we were the best of friends. Yep, two peas in a pod. So off I went to the land of swimming pools, movie stars and palm trees (with basically my enemy), what could go wrong? Of course, we had enough things to keep us loaded.

Dramatic Change of Scenery

I was in awe when I saw my first palm tree. The Spanish/Mediterranean houses with the stucco exteriors and the barrel style roofs, the manicured lawns and the people with the little dogs on leashes was cool and exciting. But for some reason, we kept driving past all of that. Then the sights changed, and for the first time in my life, I entered the Barrio.

As I said before, I came from a small town that is roughly a one by one square mile area with the population consisting ethnically of only Caucasians and African Americans. Even though Steubenville had Mafia affiliated gangsters, we didn't have gangs. My exposure to this lifestyle was about to change. The first stop was Lynwood. Lynwood is a city in Los Angeles, California and is located near South Gate and Compton, and at that time it was predominantly Latino.

I moved in with Jim's brother who lived in a one-bedroom studio apartment somewhere in that area. Jimmy and I shared a room there. During that period, Jimmy fell in love and I had to move out. Shortly thereafter, I discovered Lynwood Park and that was the beginning of my being officially homeless in California. Being homeless was nothing new to me. I have been homeless in Steubenville, so being homeless in California was easy. The weather was nice, sunny all the time, and as long as I could find something to keep me drunk or high, it didn't matter where I was. So 'urban camping' in Lynwood Park was nice.

This was my first introduction to a park bench. In the Ville, there were plenty of empty houses to squat in, but it was different out here. Plus, I didn't know the area, so the bench sufficed. Partying till you pass out makes being homeless bearable. If you can stay high, nothing mattered, and when your body was exhausted, it shut down. There were plenty of days like that, so waking up lying on the bench with my arm as a pillow was normal. I also discovered that when you are cold, you put your hands between your legs and curl up as small as possible to conserve heat. I can't remember if Jimmy gave me a blanket or someone else did, but I had one and found the many ways a blanket can serve.

I have used it to cover up with for warmth, to block the wind out when I lay under the bench, and to keep the dew off of my bottom while I slept out on the grass. Another thing that I discovered was sprinklers! Sprinklers are set on timers that usually went off in the morning. Too many days I would be awakened by water spraying out of them.

I already knew from experience that less is better. So, I hid my belongings and just wore the stuff that I had on. Wearing socks for long periods of time is okay if you don't take them off. But once you do and they are dirty, they tend to get stiff and hard to put back on. So eventually, I'd just throw them away and wear my shoes without them. However, the downside of wearing shoes without socks is that it makes your feet smell pretty unpleasant. What does it matter, if don't take them off? The embarrassing part is when you do remove them and someone is close enough to smell them!

Other individuals hung out in that park as well, and that was where I met my first gang. They were young and full of excitement. That was what I thought, but I wasn't from *the hood*; I was just some homeless guy in the park who wanted to hang out with those who knew where all the drugs were. So, I made acquaintances quickly. That alliance led me to take getting high to an entirely different level.

For some reason this gang took me in, and I got introduced to a Hispanic family where everybody hung out at their house. That's when I first discovered tortillas, burritos, tacos, and menudo. These new entrées were wonderful, but what was better was being introduced to ether-based cocaine, heroin, and a nifty juice that you soaked a cigarette in called "sherm".

During that period, I had moved into an empty house next to the drainage ditch, and this is where I lived out my insanity of Lynwood. I was taught how to inject drugs into my veins, and once that had happened, there was no turning back. I was taught what, 'coco-puffs' were (marijuana mixed with cocaine), and how to properly dip your cigarette into sherm.

Sherm is really Phencyclidine or better known as PCP, and it's classified as a dissociative hallucinogenic. So whenever I smoked sherm, I would hallucinate really badly and swear off of it forever, only to do it the next day or whenever I would come down. Cocaine back then was ether-based, and when I first injected that into my veins, it literally took my breath away. But again, if it was strong, I'd swear off of it until I came down; then I would do it again. Heroin scared me because it made me vomit and my nose would itch. I would only use small amounts of that. So, life was simple. I lived indoors, had plenty to eat, found new friends, and got addicted to more drugs. Life was so good—heck even the mailman delivered us drugs!

Nothing Really Changes

Everything stayed pretty much the same until one day, I came home and the bird that I had was gone and the house was full of smoke. What had happened was that I had met some lady that was homeless, and I allowed her to move in with me in the abandoned house I'd been squatting in. She was burning all of her identification in the sink and the smoke got so bad, she had to open the windows. When this occurred, the bird that someone had given me got out of its cage and flew the coop. This situation attracted the police, so once again I was evicted from my abandoned house due to smoke.

During that period of life, I had somehow acquired a job at a Jack-in-the-Box in Lakewood and moved into the household of someone who I was smoking marijuana with. I lived in the garage, and since I had a job, I could afford rent.

But rent plus a drug habit was expensive, so I had to supplement my income. At this fast food restaurant, I started working on the fryer. I learned how to make French fries, onion rings, tacos and breaded fish. Food wasn't a problem because we could eat at a 'discount', which meant that I stole the food and it ate for free. I eventually got promoted to the grill where I learned how to flip burgers like a pro. Cooking did great for taking care of my stomach, but what was I going to do to take care of my high?

The answer to this came soon enough. I got promoted to working the cash register. It wasn't long before I was not ringing up items but providing the customers with their purchases while I pocketed the money. This worked great, and I was on top of the world. I had food, money, a place to live, and lots of substances to stay loaded all day long. What could go wrong? Inventory!

The money didn't match the inventory, and it wasn't long before the heat was on. Guess the books weren't adding up, and I knew it wasn't but a matter of time before I would have been caught. So, before I was to be discovered, I put in and got a transfer to Costa Mesa.

I can recall these people who allowed me to live in their garage. They had cars. They were nice and allowed me to purchase their black Camaro on payments. One day I was driving down the freeway, stoned, listening to Sammy Hager's song "I Can't Drive 55." Every time the chorus of the song would say, "I can't drive 55," I would press the peddle down and accelerate 10 miles faster and sing loudly, "I can't drive **65**," then, "I can't drive **75**," and, "I can't drive **85**," etc. I was out of control when I hit, "I can't drive **115**." Smoke started to pour out of the hood and the car sputtered to a stop. I blew the engine of that car that I was buying. Well, since the car doesn't work, why should I have to pay for a broken vehicle? That could have been another reason to move.

Chapter Six
Insane Addict

Moving to Costa Mesa wasn't that bad. I had a job which gave me access to money, and the money gave me access to drugs. Upon arrival to my new place, I found the people who I needed to make my life 'normal'. When I first got to that city, the main popular road ended there at Newport Blvd, and that street is called Harbor Blvd.

It was the early nineties, and Harbor Blvd was full of action. There were prostitutes all over the place, and the hotels were as seedy as they came. Some of my favorite places to dwell were the Ambassador Inn (which has since changed names several times). There was the Tahiti Inn and a host of other places that I frequented. I used to shoplift wine from the grocery store Lucky's, which is long gone now and is currently a Ninety-Nine Cent store. On this street my addiction flourished.

Gulping down wine coolers on a hot summer day would be considered refreshing. The sweet taste of fruity artificially flavored six-percent alcohol was wonderful. Drinking a four-pack of Bartles and James was no problem. The problem normally didn't usually happen until I drank 12 bottles. Being raised with the mindset of "party till you puke" is what I believed in, and I could feel the warmth of the gastric content burn my throat. That was just part of the day, and once my stomach settled, I drank more. That was my life—drink, get sick, and then drink more. I promised that I would stop once I felt better, but that promise was just words. Even when I tried to tamper the effect of the booze with drugs, I discovered that once those got started, I couldn't stop those either. I had no problem…

Harbor Blvd. & Friends

I worked at the Jack-in-the-Box that was located on the corner of Harbor and Wilson. It was a perfect cover-up for me to steal money from and stay high while I worked. I remembered that the manager of that place was dabbling in cocaine and allowed me to move in with him, because by now, I knew all the places to get drugs, and he just didn't look like the type to be visiting some of the places that one went to acquire drugs. Plus, with his money, I could get drugs for free, so it was a no brainer for me. The only problem was that I was the type of person who would steal your drugs from you when you weren't looking and help you try to find them once they were gone. During that time period, I also sold drugs out of the drive through window to supplement my income.

This went on for a short period of time. Because of my addiction, I soon got kicked out of the house with my manager, lost my job at Jack-in-the-Box, and was back being homeless again. But like I said, Harbor Blvd was full of action back in those days, and selling drugs was my new vocation. I never felt like I belonged anywhere. I had this feeling most of my life, but out in the streets, I was part of a herd. I adjusted, adapted, and fit in like so many others do in that community, once they are there over a considerable period.

Day in and day out, I would do cocaine and spend time with the hookers on Harbor. Everybody knew my name out there, and we had a bond. There were several of us on the street. I remember when Anna used to get beat-up, and we would have to go get her from a john's car. Or when Kim would rip-off someone and go running into the alley for us to hide her. I actually watched her lose weight and just drift away to nothing but skin and bones right in from of us. I remember Sue and her husband, Allan, who was more like her pimp.

I didn't know anything about HIV, until a close friend of mine's entire family got wiped out from it. Spewey was a true and close friend to me. He took me to his home, and his mother always fed me. We got high together often, mostly marijuana and maybe some cocaine. His full name was Spewmeister J. Funkmyer III, and the memories of the times we had were priceless. His family, however, did heroin. I didn't know that in the beginning, but as time went on, I remembered watching his brother go first, then his father, and finally his mother. His brother and father weren't that close to me, but his mother sort of adopted me. She would give me shit for messing up and always lectured me on why I should be doing things with my life. Her passing was a slow one. I still remember watching her die slowly, hearing her speech slur, and finally the report of death.

I also remember Eddie who was half of the 'Bubble People.' The other half was this very bubbly lady who smiled all the time and was like a hippy. Once Eddie lit his crack pipe off of the stove because we didn't have any lighters or matches. He then passed out and hit his head on the corner of the stove. As he laid there unconscious, we decided that what he had in his pipe was probably something that was awesome, so we took it from his hand and smoked it while he was passed out.

I remember Eddie was a Deadhead and that he would take me to see the Grateful Dead with him. The thing about Dead shows was that the party in the parking lot lasted for days. We used to go to the concerts, mainly because there was plenty of acid and we could party forever. Dead shows were an experience of a lifetime. It's hard to describe the psychedelic mysticism that occurred when listening to some of the tunes that were played in the parking lot those days. When we went to the Grateful Dead show at Irvine Meadows Amphitheater, I was tripping on some crazy LSD. Once at the show in '89 I actually got on stage next to Jerry Garcia! I remembered thinking that he told me that it was alright, and I climbed over the fence. I waved at everyone and then was hauled off stage. The next thing I remember was my hands were hogtied to my feet and I was in some holding cell. They eventually released me, but that became a story that Eddie used to remind me of for years. What a long strange trip that was!

Eddie is no longer with us on this planet. May he rest in peace.

Several people allowed me to 'couch surf' back then, mainly because I knew where to get drugs and I really had no rules. I had no family, no responsibilities, and really nothing to care about. My friend Pendragon allowed me to stay at his house on several occasions, and that is where I met his sister Sally O'Malley. I remember when Hink, Maus, and Positive Paula, let me couch surf and fed me as I wandered aimless into the depths of my addiction.

Burning Bridges

I would also hang out on JoAnne Street. Behind the apartments there was a bicycle trail next to the golf course. On the other side of the course was Fairview Developmental Center. Between the bike trail and the apartments was an alley in which I spent a lot of time. We used to party there all hours of the night, then return inside to sleep. Well, it was more like when the residents of the dwelling got tired and went in. I would, too, when they would allow me, to rest and get out of the weather.

I burnt bridges fast in those days, and before you

knew it, no one was allowing me to come inside. I was in and out all the time, up all night, never slept, fighting with everyone, engaging in unwanted behavior. I was a mess, and because I was able to maintain a steady supply of drugs, people would tolerate me at a distance. They actually made me a home which was the tool shed that was built in the overhead of their carport. How ironic that I thought that it was okay to reside in a carport overhang. I never had a car but people would let me use their bikes so I could make my 'deliveries' down the trail. I think that I was beginning to be borderline delusional.

I tried to pull it together on numerous occasions. I was able to quit periodically. I worked at K-mart for a while. I remember this coin operated kiddy merry-go-round they had in the front of the store. When some kid was riding it, he hit the huge plate glass window and cracked it. I got assigned to fix the window. The glass was the length of half the store and had to be at least 20 feet high. When I was removing a piece from the bottom, I heard this vacuum sound. The entire window came crashing down on top of me! God must have been looking out for me that day. All that happened was that I got a large slice across my left shoulder (the scar is still there to this day). That job didn't last long, and I got terminated because someone found out I was drinking in the stock room on the midnight shift. I remembered the manager, Mr. White, gave me suspicious looks and the assistant manager, Marylou, had said something which gave me a clue that the jig was up. Then I got a job at the old Shell

Insane Addict

gas station but got fired because money was missing and I was the culprit. There is no doubt when I tell you that I was a liar, a cheat, and a thief in those days.

I even tried being a musician, a fantasy that I had always had since I was little and lived in the Ville. I think the first time I got a bass guitar was from Bennie, from the project days. I remember living on the streets and naming my first guitar, "Magic." I used to play it when staying at the Tahiti Inn. The memories of when Eddie used to play the drums or Pendragon would play his guitar and how we would try to jam together with the promises that one day we all would make it famous amounted to nothing, and I ended up selling Magic for some drugs. I even started writing a book back then called "Life! What About It?" and it was basically like this one. It was about my journey through life, in real time though. I had accumulated several notebooks of writings and promised all those who I was hanging out with that one day, we'd all be famous because of this thing I was scribing. But because of moving around so much, who knows what happened to those pages. I even got a job at a state hospital and was able to hide my drug use from everyone. At least I hoped I was hiding it. Or maybe I didn't care much either way. During that time, I started going to school, this was my first attempt at college, but that didn't last because I couldn't stay sober long enough to complete any tasks. Trying to understand intro to psych when you're having psychosis is difficult to say the least!

Life was bearable and meaningless. But as long as I could do my drugs and had some hustle in me, things were okay. At least that's the way it was until the phone call.

Call from Home

I did try to pull things together and was able to control my drinking and drug use. I was somewhat able to return to college and get low grades, but at least I did go to college. I think I failed everything several times, but I was trying. I was working at a state facility, when one day while I was on the floor, my supervisor approached me and told me that I had gotten a phone call from my brother. That was interesting because I had left home when I was eighteen and was now thirty-one years old. I have contacted no one from my family in thirteen years, and whenever someone would have asked me where my family was, I would lie and say that I had no one. To be honest, I had somehow successfully removed my past from my consciousness. I had not thought of my family at all. But here it was, somehow my brother had found me and was on the phone wanting to talk to me.

The conversation was that my mother was dying. I spoke to her then, and she stated that it was true, she was indeed dying. All I said was, "Okay," and that was the end of that for the moment. As I reflect on this now, I can still recall how course her voice was, how low of a tone she was speaking in. I really didn't have any feelings either way, because in my mind, this lady had been shot in the head once and made it, so she is indestructible. At that time, I had rationalized that she was tough as nails. When it came close to her actually dying, then I would do something about it. I really didn't have much time for anything back then because I was smoking crack, and that in itself was a full-time job. Two weeks later I got a second call and was told again that Mom was dying, and my response was, "Okay... let me talk to her and see for myself." This time my sister got on the phone and said that Mom didn't want to talk to me. My answer to that was, "Fine, I don't want to talk to her either." The next day the phone rang. When I answered, I was told that Mom was dead. Hearing that, something happened to me. I didn't realize this at the time, but this was the beginning to my end.

What money I had, what money I didn't have, what money I could get, by any means possible I collected. I remember making promises to people to borrow money and never having the intention of paying them back. I took blank envelopes and put them into the ATM as a deposit and withdrew money from that. I got "fronts" from drug dealers. I shoplifted alcohol and ran out of stores with booze bottles. I begged, stole, borrowed all that I could because everything went towards me wanting to blot out the world. This shell of a broken child-adult, whose false sense of reality was glued together by only denial, was starting to see a crack in his fragile world. My mother was dead, and that was the first time that I had felt anything in years. That person who I had once seen lying on the floor with a gunshot wound to her head and yet survived, was finally gone.

Unraveled

    Life as I thought I knew it came unraveled. If there was any thread that kept my sanity somewhat intact, it began to unravel. I left work that day and never returned to that job. I never went back to school either. Instead, I went and drank, smoked, snorted, injected, and ate anything that I could at that time to change the way that I felt. I couldn't get high enough to stop what I was feeling or what I was thinking. I couldn't kill myself and didn't want to live. I hated, despised, loathed, and didn't want to deal with anyone. I felt loneliness like I have never felt before, and I was so empty. Nothing could take away the pain that I felt at that time, and I could not get away from *me*. I felt as if my very soul hurt with such an intensity that even tears could not relieve it. The news of my mother's death seemed to unleash some type of hatred in me that was directed at me, and I could not turn it off. I hated myself! I was numb and didn't really care about anything or anybody at that point in time. What little money I had left, I gathered up and flew to Michigan for the funeral.

    When I arrived in Michigan, I felt isolated amongst a bunch of strangers, who were my family. My niece, Nikki, had grown into a teenager and my eldest sister, Netta, now looked just like my mother. I really cannot recall if my brother was there or not, because I was too stoned and my focus wasn't on the family. I was hurting in a way that no one around me really knew, and I just wanted to know where the narcotics were that they had given to my mother prior to her death. I was really emotionally numb to everything by then, and all I remembered was that Mom was lying there in a pink casket. I touched her and she was cold, lifeless, and dead. This was real, so very real! Although drugs filled my system, I cried. The pain was real and deep, and I could not drink or smoke that feeling away.

My mother was an only child, and her mother wasn't there. I don't know why Granny didn't show up. However, my aunts were there, and I thought that this was a good time to ask the question that I wanted to know at the moment, "Do any of you know who my father is?" The only answer that I could remember came from my aunt and she stated, "If he was the same type of father that you were a son, then it's no wonder that you two never met." That answer seared through my drug induced haze, and I can hear it ring in my ears to this day. The service was nice, and I owe this to my sisters having some weed and something to drink. I think that it was a way to keep all of us cordial for the moment. I was informed that my stepfather had passed away a couple years earlier, and that really didn't mean much to me. Even though he was a part of their family life up there, he wasn't part of mine. I fostered a resentment towards him for many years, and this was not the time for me to let it go. After all, he was the one who I had thought had shot my mother in the head all those years ago.

So, we buried her in the same cemetery that my stepfather was laid to rest, as I watched my sisters fight over who gets her rings as well as who gets what little money that she had left. My part in all of this, I just wanted to drug myself into oblivion and get the hell out of there. I didn't know anybody there, and no one really knew me. Finally, the time came when I got back on the plane and headed back to California. With me I took my attitude of 'who cares anymore?'

Arrested

Once I arrived back into Costa Mesa, life didn't really matter anymore. The damage was done, and the die was cast. I didn't even try to work and decided that I wanted to try my hand at drug dealing seriously. I fancied myself as a Robin Hood type of dealer, sell drugs to anyone who could buy them and take the money to give to those who were less fortunate. I had a grandiose vision that one day I was going to save up enough money to purchase a crack rock the size of a melon and smoke it out of a tuba. I don't know if I was geographically challenged or just paranoid, but I never made it far to peddle my goods and mainly I just hung around the intersection where Harbor Blvd. crossed Wilson Ave.—right in front of the Jack-in-the-Box in which I used to work . Back then I had a pager, and there was a payphone just outside the front door of that restaurant. That is where my experience of incarceration flourished.

Slightly east of Harbor Blvd. on Wilson Street is Wilson Park. That was my place of dwelling whenever I couldn't get a place to sleep in someone's house. I would go there and rest in the corner of the park, hidden out of sight from the street. There were days when I would just be tired from smoking crack, pass out, and come to at various times of the day, and then I'd just wander the streets. No one ever bothered me when I was down there, and that is how I lived for the moment or should I say, existed. I was always on the street, and I can imagine most people saw me wearing the same clothes repeatedly. It didn't matter back then; I didn't care what people thought.

In those days, there weren't many people out in the streets at three a.m., just the hookers, drug addicts, and others practicing all types of debauchery. However, I was one of the few. Prior to my mother dying, I was sort of shy—timid, one might say. Coming from my background, I probably would be described as an introvert. But now, I had become an angry person, and most likely, if I had been sent to see a psychiatrist, I could have won the diagnoses on antisocial behavior. But even without a proper diagnosis, I did display substance use behavior. I did have suppressed anger, and that was starting to display itself outwardly.

I once heard that the definition of insanity was doing the same thing repeatedly and expecting a different result. My behavior fit that definition, and in June of 1990, I experienced my first arrest. It was for assault and battery. I got into a fight at a party, and it got out of control. Of course, I was drunk and loaded and cannot remember exactly what happened at the party. I remember going to court, and one month later, the charges were reduced to disturbance by loud noise. I received a misdemeanor conviction and was sentenced to a work program, which I completed. But shortly after my release, I returned to my favorite spot…Harbor and Wilson.

On March 3, 1992, I was returning back from a party, and I got pulled over for looking suspicious. I appeared disheveled and spoke in some type of garbled language that didn't make much sense. I probably reeked of alcohol. Of course, I was under-the-influence, and I was arrested and released on my own recognizance. By then, I had discovered methamphetamine and was charged with possession of a controlled substance. It seems that I was becoming more delusional as time went on, but I didn't know that then, and even if I did, I didn't care about much anyway. Once I left the police station, I headed back to Harbor and Wilson.

In August of that same year, I found myself in court again. This time it was in Newport Beach, and I was being charged with assault with a deadly weapon, battery, and vandalism. This was because, once again, I got drunk and loaded on something and started fighting. I vaguely remember confronting a guy I had thought ripped off a friend of mine. I mistakenly thought he had a weapon, so I took this motorcycle helmet and hit him with it. This was the person I had become, and I now considered this normal behavior. All the charges were dismissed except battery, and that was a misdemeanor. That's when I was placed on probation and was given ninety-days of incarceration at 550 North Flower Street, Santa Ana, or better known as the Orange County Jail.

Jail

Most people would see jail as a deterrent, a lesson that you should learn that you don't want. A punishment, so to speak. But for me, it was different. After all, I really didn't care about anything anyway. What could society do to me that hadn't been done already? Being in jail at that time was almost like living in the alley, but much larger. Everyone there had attitude, and I fit right in. They gave us cigarettes in our "fish kits", and we got free food. The clothes were clean, and I didn't have to do laundry (not that I was big on laundry during this time anyway). I didn't have to get up to do anything if I didn't want to, and all I had to do was to follow some simple rules. You do as the deputies tell you to do and you go along with the politics of being an inmate. Don't get me wrong, jail isn't the place to spend your life. You must wear slippers in the shower to keep from getting fungus on your feet, the diet is limited, and you don't get to go outside much at all. There is no choice in there, and once someone starts a fight from your same ethic background, there is a chance that you would have to get involved as well. However, when I was sick in those days, jail was acceptable. I didn't feel like I was arrested, but more like rescued.

It was like a new home to me, and I was living the life of a king. In my first journey there, I remember being housed in a sixty-eight-man tank. It was like the projects, in a way, and I have been there and done that in life. But my time in my new surroundings were limited, and before I knew it, they released me for good behavior. I didn't even have to do one-fifth of my sentence and I was out of 550 North Flower. Free again, I walked the distance from Santa Ana to Costa Mesa, found a liquor store between there, got drunk and returned back to Harbor and Wilson.

    I was out of jail for a short period of time, and then once again I was in court in September of the same year. This time, in the Santa Ana court. The charges were possession of a controlled substance for sale, possession of a dangerous weapon (hammer without the head on it), transportation of a controlled substance, and possession of a controlled substance. I guess that at this time my life was really falling apart, and the courts decided to suspend the process due to my possible mental incompetence. Was I going mad? Was I finally skirting the path of insanity? Had all the partying finally caught up to me and after all these years, my cucumber was finally pickled? On the contrary, what happened was that when I was in jail, I wanted to get high so bad that I told them that I wanted to kill myself in hopes of getting some drugs. That plan back fired. Instead, they took all of my clothes, dressed me in some gown made of a thick material, and put me in a padded room for the weekend. The only place to use the bathroom was a hole in the floor. Needless to say, one weekend of that and I was cured. However, once I was released back into the main population, I got another charge for battery because I got into a fight due to some guy taking my candy bar. That netted me another forty-five days.

Endless Cycle

I really didn't care about much, and I did not have any concept of the law. My lack of knowledge of the penal system combined with my insatiable desire to want to use drugs, had me plead guilty to all the charges on November of '92 in Santa Ana court. I received a sentence of 365 days in jail (time served) and 36 months' probation with the condition of firearm restriction, register as a drug offender, and to remain abstinent from all drugs. I was released and once again, I was back into my addiction and headed back to Harbor and Wilson.

In March of 1993, I found myself in the Newport Beach court for possession of controlled substance for sale. This time I was sentenced to receive 16 months in prison. In April of '93, I walked through the gates of Richard J. Donovan Correctional Prison. I had arrived. At this point, I knew that there was a problem, and something had to be done about this. I had eight months and twenty days to contemplate what my problem was, and I was a thinker. So, while sitting in that prison yard, I finally figured out what the problem was. I was getting arrested because I didn't know how to properly conceal my drugs. So next time, I would hide them in my sock. I was released sometime around the end of that year and back into my addiction shortly afterwards. But now I was armed with facts and that hiding the stuff in my socks would be the solution. Back to Harbor and Wilson I went.

I was arrested again in 1994, in Newport Beach for assault and battery of a custodial officer, resisting arrest, and being under the influence of a controlled substance. This I remember well because I had thought that I was in a prison riot (delusion) while I was at my friend's house. The police were called because I was out of control. I received two misdemeanors and was sentenced to 36 months' probation as well as 360 days in jail. I think that my parole was violated, and I was sentenced back to prison. My plan was a success, however, because they did not find the drugs in my socks. I knew that I was on to something. This plan worked, so if it's not broke, why fix it? When I was finally paroled from Chino State Prison, I caught a bus and headed back to Costa Mesa, and once there, I went back to Harbor and Wilson.

During the month of June in 1995, I got arrested again for possession of a controlled substance and received 16 months in prison. I was found with methamphetamine in my sock and was returned to Chuckawalla Valley State Prison to complete my sentence. I was going to do at least a year, which gave me plenty of time to think about the choices I was making. I knew that something wasn't right, but I didn't know what was wrong. After spending a scorching hot summer with lizards and scorpions, I discovered what the problem was. My solution was to hide the drugs in the tiny little pocket of my jeans so that they could not be found. Yes sir, I had the answer now! I was eventually paroled from 'Chuckie's' House and went back to Harbor and Wilson.

Insane Addict

In July of 1996, I was in front of the judge in Newport Beach, charged with being under the influence of a controlled substance. They had found me hanging out at night on the streets close to Harbor and Wilson. I got sent back to prison. I was getting tired of this nonsense. I was in need of some drastic change, so I decided that this time, things were going to be completely different. I made a vow to myself that I was not going to end up in jail anymore. When I first began going to jail, the intersection of Harbor and Newport Blvd was just sand. Because I had been in jail so many times and for so long, the city had the time to build the complex Triangle Square. I needed to do some serious thinking about what was going on in my life. Once more, I came up with a brilliant fool proof idea that I know would be a great solution to my problem.

I figured that if I could keep the drugs in my hand, when the police came I could throw them away. This time when I was paroled, I did not go to Harbor and Wilson. Instead, I went one block south—to Harbor and Victoria.

I got arrested again in May of 1997, for possession of a controlled substance. I got so high that I forgot that I had the drugs in my hand, and when I was asked what I was holding on to, I opened up my fist. This time the police officer that had continued to arrest me looked at me siting in the back seat of the squad car and asked me if I wanted help. At this moment in my life, I was done. Nothing was going on. I had no life, no place to live, I really didn't even want to live. I didn't care about anything anymore. Getting high didn't even work anymore. My hustle was gone. All I could do in response to his question was to say, "Yes".

I went to jail as usual, and I did the typical routine that I always went through. My jail routine was really simple: when I go in, I shave my head, do a lot of pushups, adapt a mean scowl on my face, and then get ready to make a deal with the courts, once again, so I can get sent upstate as fast as possible.

One thing about being locked up so much is that I read a lot of books. I think that I have read all of the Louis L'Amour western novels, all of Anne Rice's novels, all of Sue Grafton's detective novels, all of Danielle Steel's books, and the list goes on. I also read the Bible, too. I even went to several Bible study groups and got certificates of completion. I used to do pushups while reciting the twenty-third psalm. I'd do fifty pushups. If I messed up a verse, I would have to start over again. It seem that God has always been with me. When my life was in a mess, I knew that I could always turn to him. It seems sometimes, everything has to be taken away from a person before the Light can shine through.

Chapter Seven
New Beginning

All my life I had always had some introduction to God. I knew that I could always cry out to Him when I was desperate. I thought that God was some entity that gave you harsh consequences when you did something bad. By looking at my life, God didn't like me much. Maybe He was upset with me for stealing money out of the church box when I was younger. Or maybe it was because of that time when I went to church and drank 10 of those little shot glasses that they pass around on the tray before you eat all the crackers. Maybe He was upset at me because when I get drunk, I preach to my homies the great things that drugs and alcohol did for me. He could be mad at me for all the lying, cheating, and stealing that I did. Yep, I know of God, and He was a punishing one for sure. But the thing that was questionable was that when I was in jail, God also gave me peace, for some odd reason.

While I was waiting to see the judge in Harbor court, I got called into the interview booth. I sat down and on the other side of the glass sat this red-haired woman with a huge smile on her face. She introduced herself, told me her name was Nancy Clark and that she was going to help me. Up until now, the people who offered me help were the ones who would give me enough drugs to sell so that I could have some extra spending money. Or they would offer me a place to sleep for a week. But I sensed that this lady meant something entirely different.

A Different Kind of Help

I had been in that holding area several times, but this was the first time that I had seen this lady. I had spoken with plenty of public defenders in my time, but she wasn't from that office. Nancy Clark was in charge of an alternative sentencing program in Newport Beach, California. I never knew that such a place existed. I was tired of living the way that I did, but I didn't know of any other solution. I was finally out of ideas. So, I told her that I wanted help. Nancy revealed to me that she knew that I had a job for the state at one point in time and that she also knew that I tried college before. This lady did her homework, and it seemed that she knew something about me.

I spent the next sixty days in jail to detox. After that, I was released into the custody of that program. I was met at the jail by a young lady named Jill H. After our 'hellos,' Jill asked me two questions that still bring a smile to my face. The first question was if I wanted a cigarette, and the next question was if I wanted Chinese food. I said yes to both. She was nice and not like the women who I had associated myself with as of late. This lady had a smile on her face and a gleam in her eye. She was friendly in a genuine way, and that caught my attention. I was suspicious of this whole deal, but I had nothing else going for me, so why not?

After the food, Jill drove me to The Recovery Center located on the edge of Costa Mesa and Huntington Beach. It was a huge apartment complex that was housed only with people who wanted to get sober or shall I say, wanted to stay out of jail. The staff at that time was: Jill, T.J., Chuck, and Dave. I remember walking through the entrance and seeing the mailboxes on the right in front of the laundry area. There were palm trees in front as you walked down the pathway and to the right, a little patio near the office area. A huge lawn area was in the center of the complex, and people were walking around happy and smiling. I felt like a stranger in a strange land. There were no palm trees and yards in *my* alley. There weren't people smiling on Harbor Blvd where I hung out. This was different for sure.

Once I got to the complex and was checked in, I was shown to my apartment. This was something completely different for me, because I had been basically homeless for years and now, I had a place to live. It was all furnished, including a kitchen with a refrigerator (even though I didn't have any money for food). I also remember Jill telling me upon my admission that if I wanted to leave this place, I should not jump over the fence, but instead walk out through the gate. This was the beginning of my new life, though I didn't know what the end results were going to be. I just knew that somehow, I could trust these individuals, and that was big. I had major trust issues and rightfully so, I had been on the streets for so long, dealing with that lifestyle.

New Style of Friends

As time went on, I met some really cool people from The Recovery Center whom to this day, I owe my life. One of which is Marnie. Marnie is down to earth and swears like there's no tomorrow. She was one of the first people I really took a liking to. When we first met, she gave me this little coin purse full of change and bought me twenty cheeseburgers, because I didn't have any money. She would also always invite me over to feed me. Marnie had red hair and always wore a baseball cap with her ponytail sticking out of the top of it. She had this huge smile that was addicting to anyone who was in close proximity to her. She also loved her dogs, and all of their names started with the letter B. I think there was Bink, Bonk, Bonzo,…

Then there was Stan. He was my first roommate and was sort of smug in his own way. Stan was probably one of the most intelligent people I had ever met in my life thus far (remember that I came from the streets). What I thought was fascinating was that he knew everything about a computer.

New Beginning

He was also the one who gave me my first computer. He also taught me how to fix them and introduced me to the internet.

Jill was the first person that I met from there. It was Jill who had picked me up and brought me to The Recovery Center, and I immediately fell in love with her. I still love Jill, and she knows it. She is one of the sweetest, kindest women that I have met, and she showed this care to all that were gifted to know her. She introduced me to Terri, who to this day, continues to remind me of when she first met me. I was in the courtyard, wearing a t-shirt and had my cigarettes rolled up in my sleeve.

Dave R. was tough and called things the way he saw it. One of his favorite statements was to refer to people as, 'Assbreaths' and 'Jaggoffs.' He also had given me the nickname of 'Antione.' Why, I don't know, but he played an important part in my journey. He also taught me about budgeting. Dave also had a sober living house in Costa Mesa, and whenever I had the need to talk to someone, his door was always open. Not only to me, but to countless other people. His favorite football team was the Pittsburgh Steelers (which is mine too), and I remember the day that he passed away. I was at his house and we watched the Steelers win the Super bowl. Shortly thereafter, he moved on to Heaven.

Then, of course, there's Nancy Clark. She was probably the kindest, strictest mother figure that anyone could have ever asked for. She was no nonsense and had no qualms about calling bullshit when she smelled it. She had strict standards that we all had to adhere to, and that was that. If Nancy didn't approve it, it just wasn't going to happen. She also had a strict dress and grooming code. To this day, she reminds all her clients the importance of being clean shaven. She was big on community service; she'd have us prepare a bunch of sandwiches and snacks to bring to the homeless community and we'd choose a retirement community to bring gifts to as well.

Inside The Recovery Center, these individuals helped set a firm bedrock in which I was able to build a new foundation that has shaped the life that I now live. These pillars have been my strength, and I owe never ending gratitude to them. I was socially inept, emotionally illiterate, and really had no positive life skills, and here is where all the grooming began. I was taught how to do simple things that people take for granted. I learned how to do chores, how to communicate without cussing, how to pay bills, and most importantly, how to deal with my anger. These people literally loved me until I knew how to love myself.

When I arrived at the Recovery Center, I was on informal probation, probation, and parole. I had no property, no money, and no real friends. I had no hope or any guidance as towards how to live life. I was physically, psychologically, emotionally, and spiritually bankrupt. But through these gates, in this environment, with these people, I changed. Somehow, it worked.

New Beginning

After a month or so when Stan moved in, he got me hooked up to the internet, and there I discovered AOL chatroom. I met a lot of online acquaintances and had created a façade that was fun in this imaginary world. That, too, netted me a close friend and confidant. In a chatroom I met Pat. Out of all the affiliates that I played with in that imaginary realm, Pat turned out to be a real friend. For some reason, we grew this bond and to this day, some twenty years later, this bond still exists between us.

It's hard for me to describe what it is that we have between us, and I guess that some may say that we are reincarnated lovers. I think that in a different world, we were married and that somehow, I messed it up, and we have been chasing each other through time ever since. Pat and I talk to each other, and I still seek her guidance in complex matters and she always end the conversation with, 'I love you.' She is one of the few in my life that lets me know that I am loved and wanted. That is something that I will forever cherish.

Now that the foundation is set and I have this new lease on life, I am ready to set foot outside of The Recovery Center and to see how life really is. I had gone ninety days so far without putting any mind or mood-altering substances into my body, and now I am tasked with going out into the community. Part of the requirement of being there was that I find employment and attend 12-step meetings. Both of these were new to me, since I hadn't done anything without using alcohol or drugs.

From Park Bench to Park Avenue

Detox

My first meeting was at a place called Charle Street (pronounced Charlie Street). Charle Street is what we refer to as a low bottom indigent detox facility, and you had to be drunk to get a bed there. It was a ten day stay, and the residents detoxed without medication. I had never paid attention to another person detoxing before (mostly due to me being on the other end), but it is a rough experience. Most of them have tremors, perspire, vomit, and lose bowel and bladder control. Even after a person has been through this experience, somehow, they still go out and do it again. I understand this fact because I had lived it myself. They had meetings inside most every day, and when there wasn't a meeting, you could go there and talk to the residents who were still in detox. There was no television and no radio. All that you had was a Blue Book of AA to read.

The first meeting I attend was the Wednesday Night Men's Stag, and that was exactly what I needed to get introduced to this design for living that would provide a road map for me to return to sanity. This group of men were just as wild as I was, but they were not drinking or doing drugs. They were sober and were boasting about how their lives were better. Plus, they were rough and rowdy, just like me. So, I was welcomed into this group.

At first, I was cautious. There was no way that the things that these people were saying were true, that their lives were unmanageable and that they recovered from a seemingly hopeless state of mind and body. But I was there and like they say, 'when in Rome, do as the Romans do.' So, I raised my hand and said what I heard them say to identify myself. Then I proceeded to tell them about how this treatment center was asking for money, how they made me make my bed and do chores, that there were rules that I had to comply with and a curfew. What The Recovery Center was asking, of course, was all unfair, and that I was trapped. After I was done with my complaints, everyone applauded me for what I just shared. I smiled and listened to the great feedback—all of them noticing how brave I was to stand up for myself.

The next person who shared was a guy named Pete. He was a big fellow. He introduced himself to the group, and then turned his focus towards me. Looking me right in the eyes he said, "You're a winey little bitch. Shut the fuck up." Everyone laughed and applauded this statement, including me. This was cool, we could talk shit to each other, and no one seemed to get mad. I liked the roughness of it all. Then he went on to tell me that I had no clue as to how to run my own life and that my best thinking got me here. He had my attention and I was riveted to almost every word that came out of his mouth. He continued to read me like a book, stating that my life was a mess and that I needed to be grateful that I have a place to live—that I wasn't still out somewhere, continuing to be a public nuisance. He also stated that I had ruined everyone's life that I encountered and that I needed a design for living that worked. He then referred to a Blue Book that had a blue covering and said that I needed to read it. This guy gave me the business!

New Style of Living

Now I really liked this place and this new style of living, so I asked this guy to help me learn this new lifestyle that he was talking about. He then informed me that he would be my sponsor and teach me about this design for living that worked for him and others. I was eager to learn and began to ask many questions. He told me to call him every day at a certain time and that if I called one minute before or one minute after this time, then he would get the impression that I really didn't want his help, and he would understand that.

In the beginning we would meet at Charle Street and read out of the Blue Book and Pete would ask me if I thought that I had any control over the amount of alcohol or drugs that I consumed or that when I start using, did I have difficulty stopping. I answered yes. Once I started, I had no way to stop, and the end results were always the same. I'd end up with no money, no hope, and eventually arrested. Then he explained to me how I had no power over my use and my life was unmanageable. At that point, I admitted that I was really an alcoholic. We learned that it wasn't my drinking that was my problem, it was my inability to react to life the way it presented itself. I had to learn to accept that this was a fact and admit this to myself—way down deep in my soul. That was the moment that I had surrendered and started to realize that I had a fatal disease that would kill me if I didn't do something about it.

New Beginning

I went back to The Recovery Center where Dave was working and told him of what I had just learned, about Pete and about this first step into my new beginning. Dave listened to me and when I was done, he looked me in the eye and said, "That's good, Assbreath".

Now these gatherings of people who talked about not drinking or doing drugs were all over the place. They are referred to as fellowship. They were in churches, in homes, in institutions, and even in clubs. They were available all hours of the day and sometimes all night. I went to these places for several reasons—first of all Nancy required them. and second of all, so did Pete. After a while, I liked going, and eventually people started to know my name. They were really friendly, and I fit in. I created a daily routine for meetings so that I could belong to the fellowship. I went to the club for the morning meeting, the church for the noon meeting, and then back to The Recovery Center for our evening group. Life was good, and I hadn't had a drink or a drug for at least ninety days. Hell, I could do this all day long. Until one day, Nancy told me that I had to get a job.

Employment wasn't really my cup of tea at that time. I was a hustler, a two-bit drug dealer. At that point in time, the only thing that I could say I knew for sure was that twenty-eight grams made an ounce, and if you mixed baking soda with cocaine, you could make a crack rock. Not the best thing to put on a job application. Plus, I was scared. I had not used any mind-altering chemicals for ninety days, and I didn't want to leave the confines of The Recovery Center. So,

I asked Nancy if I could just be the gardener there. Nancy wasn't having that. She said that I had to go work and pay my way like the rest of the world and that I would be fine.

Power Greater Than Myself

Eventually I did find my first job, and it was telemarketing for point of sales terminals. I incorporated that into my daily routine while continuing to go to meetings. I went to work and went to group. As life progressed, so did my work with Pete. He showed me that since I was powerless over my life and my choices to do the right thing, I would have to find some type of power that could help me stay sane. I questioned him about the 'sane' stuff. He told me that judging by the way that I had described my drinking and drugging, I would choose booze and dope over eating, family, living indoors, and taking care of myself, therefore I was insane. Well, he had me there, so he instructed me on how to find a Power greater than myself that could restore me to sanity.

I remembered that as a child my mother would take us to church. I remember when she used to lick a cloth and wipe the crud off my face with it. How embarrassing is that? I remember sitting in the Second Baptist church and having to sit still while the sermon was going on, and how I anxiously waited for the crackers and grape juice to come in those little cups. I was taught to pray from early on, but I really didn't know what I was doing. It was more like paying lip service and doing what I was told. I knew that when my ass was in deep trouble I could pray. I knew that all those times I was in prison, I prayed every day. So, I was familiar with seeking out God.

Pete also told me that a book could be a power greater than myself, a judge could be a higher power, or that God could be the ultimate Power, if I wanted it to be. So, I started praying everyday as instructed. At that time, he had me create a list of three things that I was grateful for every day. He told me to call it my gratitude list. I discovered that I was grateful for water, food, shelter, clothes, teeth, toothpaste, electricity, air—hell, I was grateful for everything! Everything except one thing. I wasn't grateful that I had to give all of my money to Nancy for rent.

By the time that I got a check from telemarketing, I would just sign my name to the back and hand it over. Nancy, up until this point, had given me a scholarship, and I had to pay her back. I didn't mind, except that I didn't have any money left and that sucked. I mentioned this to Dave, and he stated, "Why don't you cash your check and keep fifty bucks for yourself, Assbreath?" Yep, at that time, I was taught how to budget. At this time in my life, I had no clue about how to manage money, and it was Dave that gave me my first introduction to money management.

My life after that was pretty much a routine. I'd get up in the morning and pray, read my gratitude list, go to a meeting, go to work, come home and eat, go to a meeting, go to group, eat dinner, then go to bed. This pattern went on for months, and in the midst of all of this, Pete was guiding me through that Book. I had discovered that turning my life over to God was the best thing that I could do, and it really didn't matter what my own personal perception of God was. Pete wasn't really strict on what I believed in, as long as I wasn't the one who was in charge of my life any longer.

I was learning things like how to make a list of all of my liabilities and assets. If I found something that was useful to my new-found growth, then I could keep it. If it stopped my growth, then I had to remove it out of my life. Or at least, let it go and allow God to take care of it. This was learning to surrender, and it wasn't really that bad. At that time, I had way more bad stuff than good, things which I thought were essential to life and that I could never give up. Resentments were not good for me. Hanging on to them would cause me more harm than good, but I wanted to keep them because they allowed me to have justifiable anger. He insisted that I search deeply for them and let them go, because they were killing me. Pete explained that resentments were like drinking poison and waiting for the other person to die.

Pete also taught me that it was okay to admit my faults to other people and to talk to God. It was ok to remind myself of what my wrongs were and not just in a sugar-coated way but being honest about it.

Freaking Out

As I stayed away from drinks and drugs, I started accumulating time sober. I was about six months without anything at this time, and life was groovy. Until this one day. I was in our apartment with Stan and Lenny. Lenny wasn't really serious about staying sober, and I had a suspicion that he was nipping the bottle. But I didn't care, it wasn't my business. I had learned by then that I could not make anyone stop drinking, so I just let them do whatever they wanted. However, on that day, Lenny was watching television while sitting on a lazy-boy recliner, relaxing. There was a coffee table at the foot of the chair and there was a little space between the two. I was walking past him to get to the door but decided to take a short cut between the coffee table and the bottom of the chair. While doing so, I accidentally brushed my leg against the bottom of the chair. For some reason, this upset me, so I slapped Lenny in the face.

    I freaked out! I could not believe that I had hit him. I didn't know why I did it, I just did. I wasn't so much worried about getting kicked out of The Recovery Center, but I was shocked that I was that volatile. I had been there six months without any problems, and I felt that my life was on track. I messed up! Both of us were brought up to the counselor's office where I cried and apologized for what I did. I really couldn't believe that I went off like that. Lenny accepted my apology and stated that he forgave me, saying that he understood because I just reacted to what I knew. Hearing that this was the only way I knew how to act sort of pissed me off again. But I contained myself and went back to the apartment. I told Dave about it that night, and he just said I was being a 'Jaggoff' and needed to go to a meeting.

I met with Pete the next day and explained what I had done. He made me read something out of the Book and told me that I had to figure out a way to get rid of these character flaws. He stated that I should make a list of them all and get ready to be rid of them. The fighting, the anger, the resentment, the lying, the cheating, the stealing. Then he said to add the seven deadly sins, too, in case I missed some things. So, I listed 'wrath, greed, sloth, pride, lust, envy, and gluttony' as well. He instructed me that once I am done with those, I was to get on my knees and pray for God to remove them from me. I wanted to say, "What an order! I can't go through with that," but I knew Pete's answer would have been, "Are you willing to go to any lengths to stay sober?"

So, I moved forward with my progress. I was committed to living this new lifestyle. Things got better and better. I took on commitments, went to meetings early and stayed late. I started to learn things about myself that I never knew before. I discovered that I was a selfish little boy living in the body of an adult. What was more important than anything was that I had to admit that this was me, and I had to take a long hard look at myself.

Facing My Flaws

Some of my flaws were glaring and easy to spot. I looked forward to taking care of them so that I could have more of the relief that I have been getting. Learning how to let things go and not taking things personally was not that much of a challenge. I learned that when I was in a confrontational situation, there were certain cues and events that triggered me, which could lead me to anger. I learned the difference between anger and hostility. Anger is a normal emotion that is okay to feel, but hostility is an action that is taken with consciousness of thought. Whenever I found myself getting agitated for too long or too frequent, it was a warning to change the situation. I learned to walk away, and that helped with the wrath part of my character flaw.

When I didn't want to get a job, it pretty much meant that I was lazy. This was sloth. I thought that since I was a hustler (that took a lot of effort), there was no way that I was slothful. Pete reminded me that I never had a real job, and that I was complaining about cleaning up after myself when I was asked to do chores. His remedy to this was that I had to make up my bed every day in the morning and that I could never leave a job until I had a better one to replace it. He also informed me that since I smoked, I was the man who had to volunteer to wash the ash trays after each meeting.

Working on pride was fun. There wasn't much I was too proud of! Yet, I did have a false sense of pride, because I had been on a roll with my life and felt invincible. Pete reminded me of when I hit my roommate, and that I really didn't have it all together. He stated that the things that I do, I need to give credit to God for, because He allowed me to have these experiences, and there is nothing that I do on my own. Even though I did the footwork, God—not me—was responsible for the results. Between them both, my ego was getting busted left and right. He also told me that the acronym for E.G.O. meant Edging God Out, and that I must practice humility daily. This is why I should always pray on my knees—to humble myself.

Gluttony was explained to me like this: I should not want for more than I could handle and to be grateful for the things that I have. I learned that more is never better and that sometimes a little bit of something is better than whole lot of nothing. He explained that all of this stuff is God's and that He allows us to use it while we are here on earth. I cannot take anything with me, so why waste things that He gives us?

These lessons were ground into my head. I know that there were seven deadly sins he said to work on. I wish I had paid attention to the three that I must have ignored: greed, envy, and lust.

Chapter Eight
Slip & Skirt

I thought that I had everything under control. Not a cloud in the sky, I knew that I had nothing to worry about. I was cocky and sure of myself and laughed at those who relapsed back into their assorted addictions. It wasn't me, and I was on the steady road to redemption. My chest was plumped with pride, and I was invincible. Going to meeting was good enough for me, and everything I heard sounded groovy. Once, in a meeting, I heard the phrase, 'underneath every skirt lies a slip'. I find that to be one of the many aphorisms that I have picked up throughout the years. In my case, this happened to be true. One day without any effective defense, I found myself strung-out once again.

Going Wrong

While my life was moving forward, I had amassed the

total of eighteen months of being drug and alcohol free. This new pattern of living was working, and my life was great. I was working, going to school, and enjoying life. I had a host of new friends that I could depend on. I had places to be and was welcome in circles that felt like home. My new life was filled with transformation, and I called that recovery. I had a new-found hope and was no longer in that state of hopelessness of mind and body. I found that if I continued to help others like those who had helped me, put my reliance on God and others who were more qualified to make decisions for me, my life would be a success. What could go wrong at this point? Well, something did go wrong.

One day while I was walking across the street to get doughnuts for our weekly Sunday morning meeting, I ran into the wife of an old friend of mine. She was a sight to see because I hadn't seen anyone from the Old Days yet. We struck up a warmhearted conversation. She was giving me the latest news on everything, and I listened with great intent. She finally ended by telling me that this buddy of mine needed to have a court card signed, stating that he was attending meetings. Well, being the secretary at my meetings, I thought I could help him and talk to him about this new way of life that I had experienced. I hoped that maybe one day, he too could have this experience that I was having. She informed me that they lived close by and that I should come over and visit. I agreed and we parted our ways for the day.

About a week later, I showed up at my friend's house and was welcomed in. There were lots of people there and when we met, it was like a family reunion. We chatted about the good times that we had when we used to run amuck. We talked about all the people who we knew that were incarcerated and those still doing all the forms of debauchery out there in the community. It was exciting for me to be in this environment, and I was caught up in the moment. We had our conversation about this new form of life that I was having, and my friend was excited that I had turned over a new leaf in life. He wished me well and I departed.

    I continued to go to my meetings and applied myself to my new job. I was passing my classes in school, and things were still on the upswing in my life. So, more and more I would do my daily routine, but added a new element into the mix. I started to visit my friend more and more. So much so, that my visits became a daily routine. The more that I visited him, the more that would we talk about the old lifestyle that I once lived. The more we talked about that, the more I missed those days. The more I missed those days, the more I forgot to discuss my new life and longed for the old one. My new life now appeared dull, not glamorous, but less exciting. I was really a small fish out there in society; a broke telemarketer with a curfew. Sure, my new acquaintances were okay, we went to meetings and drank coffee and talked about how grateful we were. However, here at my friend's house was action! Fast times, fast women, and quick money with no rules in sight. Chaos and debauchery were presented in spades! What a contrast to what I was currently receiving, and that awoke something in me that felt familiar. What I later discovered was that this is what envy felt like.

Downhill Fast

In the following weeks, the company that was at my friend's house started to get to know me better. My friend and I were close, and there were times that he would give me his money to hold, stating that he trusted me better than those around him. This made me feel special, and others there started to treat me with some type of reverence. As time went on, I was trusted with holding the drugs, too. I was the only one in that environment that was really sober, and of course, I wasn't going to use the drugs. I was feeling like I was somebody special, and the power behind that was enormous. Greed was starting to set in, and I didn't even know it at the time.

After a while, I was living two different lifestyles. By day, I was hanging out with my friend, being this trusted confidant of a drug dealer, and then by nightfall, I was into the recovery scene. It was a mixed-up world for me. I was soon to discover that when you hang out at the barbershop, eventually you're going to get a haircut!

One day I was hanging out at my friend's place, and there was this particular female that was coming over for drugs on a regular basis. She was cute and addicted, and I would watch her inject drugs into herself and come alive sexually. My current life was bland. Meeting, work, school, no excitement at all, not like what was going on in front of me. I missed that life and wanted a piece of the action. This woman was sitting front of me on this particular day, and I was chatting up a storm with her. She went on with her business just as casual as anyone else would. As we talked, she pulled out her syringe, spoon, and her methamphetamine and started to mix it up. She was wearing a skirt that day and it must have been hot because she wasn't wearing any panties. She must have noticed me looking at her and she smiled, leaning forward with spoon in hand, opened her legs and asked me if I wanted some? I can't even recall having an effective mental defense to this but simply smiled and nodded my head… yes. I recognize that last character defect (sin) that I didn't take care of, but at this point, it was too late.

Methamphetamine is a powerful stimulant, and it was my last drug of choice. I took that syringe-filled drug, injected into my veins, and felt alive and paranoid, all at the same time. I also felt guilty. But it was too late. I had relapsed, and that's all there was to it. No one is to blame for this relapse but me, and the truth of the matter is that I had set myself up for this long before I ever took that drug. There was no turning back once the gorilla was out of the cage.

My spiral downhill was fast. Before you knew it, my grades in school were sagging, so I dropped out again. The side effects of the drugs were apparent. I was losing weight, had no appetite, my hands were always trembling, and I was sweating all the time. I was exhibiting increased paranoia and had mild psychotic symptoms (I remember seeing bushes turn to people and engaged in meaningful conversation with them). It was becoming harder to hide these symptoms when I went to my meetings. My solution? I started going to less meetings. I would stay up late and miss my appointments at work, so I got fired. I needed income, so I started dealing drugs again. The difference was that I was part of a sober living community and swore that I was abstinent. One thing at least that I had learned from my previous experience was that I was to stay away from Harbor Blvd.

My life had quickly gotten miserable. I wasn't eating, barely sleeping, and trying to hide my relapse from everyone. The proverbial gorilla was out of the cage and it was kicking my butt. I hated life but couldn't stop. I started going around more of the old crowd and less time was spent with my new friends. My meetings were getting short, and I had stopped praying all together. I was dehydrated most of the time and stayed up late at night, because I couldn't sleep. I wished that there was some end to all this madness. All I wanted to do was to get sober again, and I couldn't. I was sick and tired of being tired and sick.

March 29, 1999

The date was March 29, 1999—the day that I will remember for the rest of my life. I was sitting in my car and waiting to deliver some drugs to a stranger in Riverside, California. I remember that I had to pray, because the emotional pain was overwhelming. I had learned that God would do for me what I could not do for myself and that I should ask with no reservations for His protection and care.

I knew that God would do this, if I sought Him. So, I asked God for help one more time with complete abandon.

On the way to Riverside, I was pulled over in my car for having a broken taillight. I was with a girlfriend of my connection, and when we got pulled over, I was pulled out of the car. There was a suspicious container in the back seat of the car, and when the police officer asked me what was in the container, I simply told him, "a little meth." I was done. All full of guilt, shame, remorse, and embarrassment, emotionally spent and spiritually bankrupt. Finally, the madness was stopped. I have always known that once my addiction gets started, the only way to stop it is to be physically removed from society—whether it be in some type of institution, jail, or for some, death.

That 'little meth' turned out to be 67 grams of methamphetamine, and once again, I was taken to jail. This was the first time that I was incarcerated in Riverside, but jail is jail. I was glad the madness had stopped but not happy about being in a strange place of confinement. I was accustomed to being at the Orange County Jail and had a lot of friends back there. Here, in Riverside, I was a stranger in a strange land. I remember that when they told me about my charges, the first offer from the courts was to do eighty percent of a 12-year prison term. I felt like, "Holy crap! You really screwed this up, Anthony!" I told my public defender at the time that I was intoxicated still and that I had no clue about what they were talking about.

Once my mind was a little clearer, I called Nancy to inform her of what had happened. She told me that she knew because the joint task force came and raided the sober living place that I was residing in. I was embarrassed because this is the person that gave me a new life and I had failed! On the phone, Nancy told me that she understood why I did what I did, and the only thing that I'd have to do is get back into working a program and start a new sobriety date. I really don't know what I felt back then about her words, but to think that someone forgave me for screwing up my life was new to me. She also asked me to write an autobiography of my life and send it to her. I got back into praying again, and asked God for forgiveness and to enter my life again. I wrote the letter that Nancy asked of me, and God inserted His will into that quickly.

Returned to Sender

When I wrote the first version of my autobiography, I ended it with my driving to Riverside and getting pulled over with some drugs that belonged to the girl that I was with, and that I was taking the wrap for her. That letter got returned to sender because of the lack of postage. The second version was the entire truth, with me owning everything and blaming no one. That letter made it through to Nancy. I went to court shortly after, and Nancy came and represented me. She was able to convince that judge that I was a broken human being and that I should be given another chance at life. The judge agreed and sentenced me to almost three years in prison. When I was asked by the courts if I had anything to say, I stated, "Thank you, Your Honor," and that I was an alcoholic. The judge in turned replied, "Well son, I guess you have plenty of time to sober up."

My life was so different this time around. I felt a peace that was always around me and a sense of freedom, even while I was locked up. God and I got close, and I received several certifications from the Bible classes I attended. One day, while I was walking the yard at Chino, I found a Bible that was in the trash can (which I still have to this day). It was covered in all sorts of stuff, and I took good care of it. The pages were all stuck together with assorted fluids, and I took my time and pealed all the pages apart and dried each of them. There are some marked areas by someone who must have used it, and every now and again, when I would be talking to God, the wind would blow open a page and the message would be right in front of me. During those days, I finally got baptized for the first time in my life.

At that point in time, I started journaling. I have found that this gives me a way to get things out of my head and into reality. This also allowed me time to openly communicate with God. I still have that journal and can see how I was talking to God every day and the proof He gave to me that He was listening. Most of the writing was about giving thanks and how grateful I was to be alive. I wrote about everything that I encountered during that time period. I mostly journaled about spiritual warfare and different passages from the Old Testament. When I looked through those pages these days, I get a chance to see how unmanageable my life was when the madness finally ceased. I can see where God was working in my life then and still is to this day. It's important for me not to forget those days, so I keep that book with me, and from time to time, I pull it out to get a glimpse of what life used to be like.

Chapter Nine
Road of Happy Destiny

A New Road

God will do what you cannot do for yourself. I prayed with complete sincerity to stop the pain that had returned to me. I know that He could save me if I was honest and from what I had learned, He does answer prayers. I found a relationship with God, a true relationship that gave me a life, and I knew deep in my heart that God was still in the miracle business. I remember going to my knees in tears, because I completely surrendered myself to Him. Thus started my Road of Happy Destiny.

My life, as I see it today, started on March 29, 1999. That is also the last time that I have ever taken a mind-altering or mood-altering substance into my body. I can say truthfully that I haven't had a drink of alcohol or taken a drug since then. I have also revisited those seven deadly sins and work constantly to deal with them all.

My world has changed a lot since those days of past, and I have improved remarkably. I know that there is a correlation between not drinking and using and the life that I lead today. But starting from this point wasn't easy. Or should I say, it took a lot of work.

So here I was, a felon in the eyes of the law, with an eighth-grade education, a box of letters from prison, homeless, unemployed, and with really no social skills. I set out on this journey which has led me to this book.

Nancy had picked me up from Chino Prison, sometime in December of 2001, and took me to her sober living place in Costa Mesa. It was an apartment complex close to College Hospital, and that's where my new journey began. Gino was the manager there at that time, and I remember seeing some of my personal belongings in his garage. I could say that he had stolen my things, but in all honesty, I gave my belongings up when I chose to use and drink again. Now this was my new beginning, and resentment was a luxury that I could not afford. He was pleasant to me, but stern, and we butted heads from time to time.

It was gravely important that I not relapse on any behaviors, so I learned to restrain my tongue. If I listened to the things that my brain was telling me, I should share these thoughts with other people. My head, as I have learned at this point, was not a reliable source for information. So, I got back into the fellowship, found a sponsor to sort out my thinking, and began to focus on the future, not the past. I learned the Serenity Prayer years ago, and this came in handy for almost anything that I found myself in direct conflict with.

Shortly thereafter, I remember seeing Dave again, and he informed me that he had a friend that worked at a well-known treatment center in Tustin called Cornerstone and that he would take me down and introduce me. That is when I met Lynda and Maggie. They introduced me to Dr. Stone, who owned this place, and pleaded my case to him, which led to me being hired there as an office person and house manager. Here was another example of God doing for me what I couldn't do for myself. He opened doors that I had no idea were even there. I also came to understand that God doesn't have to show Himself in an elaborate way. He does a lot of work through people. As a house manager, my rent was free, and I received a small stipend for working there as well. At this time in my life, I decided to go back to school and finish up some of the things that I had always tried to accomplish, but was unable to because of my disease of addiction.

Making amends and cleaning up the wreckage of my past is what I had in mind. I wanted to make right all the wrongs that I had done. Getting and keeping a job was my new mantra and finishing school was the other. I was taught how to make and keep a commitment, as well as responsibility and accountability by washing the ashtrays and cups at Charle street. I also knew that there were no more shortcuts in life, so if I was getting paid to do a job, I had to give my best to what was in front of me.

During this time, I was on parole and had to check in from time to time, but I was doing well. I enrolled in Cypress College and started finishing up the Psychiatric Technician program. I had tried to do this program several times in the past, but never could get past first semester. However, this time I was armed with the facts about my recovery, and I knew that if I would put the same amount of effort towards my life I did in all of those years of drinking and drugging, then I could have a fair chance of being successful.

Most of the instructors there remembered me and welcomed me back in. I attended my classes with vigor. The first semester was nursing science (the class that I am blessed to be teaching currently), and that is where the information about making mitered corners was finally grasped. So did feeding, medication administration, and the rest. Also, at this time, Cornerstone had started to host an addiction class at their outpatient facility, and I signed up for it. I started attending those classes every Saturday, and in the end, I became a Certified Addiction Specialist (CAS). So there I was, going to two schools, and having a job with a nice place to live. Cornerstone and its staff truly did play an important part in my journey.

One day during this period, on the way to see my parole officer, I received a phone call from Lynda. I cannot remember the entire conversation, but I do remember that during the call, she mentioned something to the effect of wanting to have a dual diagnoses program within her facility. I told her that I would create one for her. I had not gotten into any trouble and had just petitioned for early release from parole. I was granted this and for the first time in ten years, I finally had no adult supervision.

Cleaning Things Up

Once I got off parole, I had to take care of all the legal stuff that I got involved in. Cleaning up the wreckage of my past was needed. I had a long history of legal issues, which meant that in society, I was a convicted felon and ex-parolee. Getting work was hard and working in treatment was okay, but what if I wanted to work someplace else? What's more, how could I practice in the healthcare industry with a history of extensive substance use? I prayed about this matter and asked for God's will. Either I was meant to work in healthcare or not, that's not up to me.

The first step was for me to write to the Department of Justice and get a copy of my RAP sheet. Once I got that in the mail, I read it and felt embarrassed. I knew of what I had done (I lived it), but to see it all in front of me on paper was something entirely different. This was a lot, but the work had to get done. First thing I had to do was to go to every police station and courthouse that I have had the pleasure of visiting, and get copies of the outcome of all my transgressions. That took time, money, gas, and yes, lots of determination. All of the felonies that didn't land me in prison had to get reduced down to misdemeanors, and the misdemeanors had to be dismissed.

Part of my new life was making right all the wrongs that I had done. This included going to the Costa Mesa police department and apologizing for the crimes that I had done to this city. I sought out and met the same officer that had arrested me numerous times and told him of my new life and that I was sorry for the things that I had done. He stated that if I were living a different lifestyle, then my apology was accepted. I was relieved because I had to make several amends to different entities, so I was getting the hang of it. The best part of this was that I was no longer worried about visiting police stations or court houses now, because I was able to walk in and leave of my own free will. This allowed me to put this part of my life behind me.

After all of the paperwork was filed (it was as thick as a college textbook), it was to be presented to the judge. I consulted my brother who told me that I shouldn't represent myself. But I was on limited funds. I was stuck between making too much money to qualify for the New Leaf legal aid program and not enough money to pay for a good attorney. Nancy was really helpful and introduced me to someone who guided me. So, I was pretty much on my own. Onward I went.

Since I had done time in prison, getting my record expunged was out of the question. The next best thing was to get a Certificate of Rehabilitation, then wait for a pardon from the governor. In order to get a Certificate of

Rehabilitation, I had to prove beyond a reasonable doubt that I was a changed man. I had to gather a ton of documents to show that I was, indeed, not the person in those preceding chapters.

The documents I prepared for the courts included: the resolved court cases, my work evaluation for 2 years of employment, income taxes from past 6 years, and 50 letters of reference. I remember taking all of this to superior court for the first time and the judge told me that I didn't complete the paperwork, and the district attorney wouldn't accept the package. I stated that I understood and requested copies of the minutes from the court to see exactly what I missed. Then I thought I corrected it. I returned one month later. Again, the same judge, in the same court room, rejected my package. Off I went to the clerk's office to get the transcripts of the hearing, then home to readjust the package, and then back to court once again to present my case. Either persistence paid off, the courts were tired of seeing me, or God opened the door, because the third time was the charm and sometime during December of 2009, I was granted my Certificate of Rehabilitation from the state of California

C.A.R.E.

As a student in the psychiatric technician program at Cypress College, I met young lady named Victoria, who was feisty and intelligent. I told her of the idea of me creating a dual diagnoses program for this treatment center and she agreed to help me. We were just students at the time and put our brains together, and we came up with C.A.R.E.

Being the godparent of a program—now that I think about it—is awesome. I was there from its conception and am still with it today. C.A.R.E. was conceived in 2002 by two Cypress College Psychiatric Technician students, Anthony Brown and Victoria Yates. It is designed to help individuals that have mental illness and substance abuse disorders get help with living life. Victoria basically gave me guidance and feedback while I wrote and implemented the program. The first C.A.R.E. groups were held in the garage at one of the houses that Cornerstone owned. Dr. Stone was very supportive of this project and nurtured it along as we developed. At that time, it was only for males, and we only had eight beds. The house was large, and we had a manager (me) and an assistant manager. We had a swimming pool for the individuals, and we supplied food and transportation for all our clients.

All the clients were dual diagnosed, so we got to manage medications and behaviors. I purchased all of the computers for this program and wrote all of the curriculum for the groups that I lead. Pat, from the AOL chatroom that I had met years prior, had an associate of hers create our blue heart symbol (see our website: www.caredd.org) and C.A.R.E.'s mission statement. This was the first time I was in management, but I had no title then. The idea grew and so did the client base. We started up a female house and began marketing for it. We hired more staff and things were moving along great.

The acronym for C.A.R.E. today stands for Coordinating & Assisting Recovery Environments, but when I first created this program for that treatment center, it stood for something else. But never-the-less, within a year, this program grew from having an eight bed men's house, to becoming a valuable aftercare support entity. During this time period, the drug, Suboxone came out. It was supposed to be the answer to methadone when it comes to opiate/opioid addiction. It is considered a mixed agonist-antagonist class of drug. I remember that Cornerstone was first when it came to studying this drug's effect, and I was providing controlled groups with this medication at the time. I found that fascinating and valuable information to have and again, give thanks to Dr. Stone for allowing me this experience.

    I continued to complete my classes at Cypress College and graduated in 2003. I went on to get my license from the state of California to practice as a Psychiatric Technician. I came to understand that if I took a couple more classes, I could get another degree. So, I finished all of my general education classes and received my Associates in Arts for general education. I then applied and received my Associates in Science Psychiatric Technician degree. So here I was, with two degrees, one counseling certificate, a dual diagnoses program under my belt, off parole, and working at a good job. This was all within four years. Life was wonderful, but I still had a lot of catching up to do. I was far behind everyone else in my age group, and I just wanted to move forward.

    I left that treatment center in 2005, because I had met a woman there who I wanted to build a life with. She was working for the same company, and we both decided to leave, move in together, and get married. We really didn't know each other well, but I thought that we could grow to love one another and things would end with living happily ever after. We both were in recovery and at that time, I had saved up a lot of money because I didn't have to pay rent for several years. My idea was, since I had some money and she had great credit, we could get married and buy a house. We did, but within less than a year, we decided that it would be best if we got a divorce. We came from two different walks of life, and things were just not working.

Sadness and Hope

She moved out, and I paid her for her half of the house. I still live in this place. I remember when she left. There was nothing here because most of the stuff was given to us by her relatives. She took her belongings, and after the dust was settled, the only thing that remained in this two-bedroom house was a mattress and box spring, four dressers, a refrigerator, a television, two book cases, and a matching couch and chair. There were no pictures on the wall, no curtains, no appliances, and one set of sheets. And, of course…me.

I really felt devastated after that loss. I was now working at Anaheim General Hospital in their psychiatric department. I'd work, come home, and be sad, because I was all alone. I remember crying on one occasion, holding my ex-wife's bicycle helmet. My life was miserable. But during that time, I didn't want to drink alcohol or do anything to damage or hurt anyone. I was at a strange place, and the only thing that I wanted to do was pray and go to meetings. So, I did. I remember going to a meeting, and sharing about my divorce and how much it hurt. I remember being at this meeting, sharing, when this elderly lady by the name of Betty approached me. She kissed me on the cheek, patted my face, looked me in the eye, and said, "You know, Honey, divorces are tough. I've had four of them… you'll get used to it." At that moment, I knew that God had heard me, and my pain was replaced with a smile. I knew what I needed to do, so I got busy living life.

One day when I was at work, I noticed that some of my supervisors were treating the housekeeper unfairly. Her name was Berta. When she wasn't around, they would make mean statements about how she was not the same as them, that she was less educated and poorer. After hearing this for a while, I decided to give them a piece of my mind. I basically told my supervisors that if they didn't start treating her with respect, then when we are on the floor, I would not intervene with the clients when they started to have aggressive behavior. It's interesting to be six-foot one, weigh two hundred and fifteen pounds, and have years of street smarts. For some reason, all of the clients that I worked with in the mental hospital seem to get along with me. I guess they recognize their own. The supervisors started being nicer to her, and one day, I asked Berta if she wanted a side job of cleaning my house. She accepted, and from that point forward, I have had a housekeeper. However, this isn't just some ordinary housekeeper. This lady helped me put my personal life back in order. Unfortunately, she passed away a couple of years ago from liver disease, but she had made an impact in my life.

As I sit in my house, I still feel the memories of her every day. The paintings that are hung on my walls were placed by her and her husband. The drapes that cover the windows of my patio doors are from them. Years later, her husband and daughter still come by to help me out. To tell you the truth, I don't know what I would do without them. I smile when I tell people that I have lived in my house for over 15 years, and I have only vacuumed my carpet maybe five times at the most. I don't ever remember cleaning my bathtub or moping a floor at home. Come to think of it, I have never washed the shelves of my refrigerator, washed any of the windows, or polished furniture in my place. I guess that's what happens when you have had a housekeeper for the past 15 years.

Thinking back in time, I can still recall that there were days before all of this when I was sitting outside in the rain because I had no place to go, and no one wanted me around. I can still recall eating old cheeseburgers out of a dumpster (taking the tomatoes and lettuce off first, of course), because I was so hungry. I can remember having to wear the same clothes for several days, if not weeks, at a time. Now, I look around and have not only a house, but a housekeeper to keep it clean. Talk about a stark difference!

Chapter Ten
Education is the Key

With all of the skipping of school I did when I was younger, and having to repeat grades, I barely made it to the ninth grade and then dropped out. I only say ninth grade because I spent three years in the seventh grade and two years in the eighth grade. I finally made it out of Grant Jr. High because I was getting too old for them to keep me there any longer, and I spent just one day in high school.

My philosophy back then was that I didn't need an education, because I was going to make a living out of being a drug dealer. I thought that the only knowledge that I would need was that twenty-eight grams made an ounce and that's what was needed to make money. I knew how to fight and only that was needed for survival out on the streets. I guess that was good for then, but those skills really could not be used in my new life as a sober adult. So, education is what I needed.

Committed to Completion

When I was in the county jail, I was able to take classes that allowed me to get my GED. That was my starting point. When I started college, my goal was to complete the things that I started with. So, the first classes I took led me towards becoming a psychiatric technician. What made me think about being a psychiatric technician in the first place? Well, I once had a job as a janitor at a developmental center. I saw all kinds of people there as I was cleaning floors, scrubbing toilets, and washing all kinds of things off the walls. I noticed many staff members interacting with the clients. I didn't like what I saw—the way they talked to them, treated them overall, and I thought that I could do a better job working with these individuals. But what could I do? I was into my disease and semi-psychotic myself. I thought about all of this now, being a new person, so I made a commitment to finish the things that I had started. I went back to school to study this course.

Returning does require a commitment and sacrifice, and for me to be successful, I had to have both. Working full time and going to school full time was a challenge, but I was driven, so whatever sacrifices were needed, I made them. School requires homework, paperwork, study time, classroom time, and for the courses that I was taking, clinical time. So, where was the fun time? Well, that would have to come later. I was fortunate because my rent was covered while I was at the treatment center, which lasted through most of the tech program. But I didn't get much for a stipend, so I applied and received a Pell Grant during this portion of my education.

The Psychiatric Technician program is a three-semester course, plus prerequisites of Integrated Medical Science and Introduction to Psychology. I completed those courses and entered the program. The first semester went smooth. I completed Nursing Science I, Nursing Science II, and Developmental Psychology. That is where I learned the basic skills of nursing. I learned vital signs, activities of daily living, and a host of other things that made me qualified to enter the field of health care. During that period, I received my first certification as a Certified Nurse's Assistant.

I moved forward into the program. The second semester consisted of Developmental Disabilities I and Developmental Disabilities II. In those classes, I was trained in the use of behavior modification techniques. I smile when I tell my friends that I can make an apple believe that it's an orange just based on the principles that they are both pieces of round fruit.

The third semester consisted of Mental Disabilities I, Mental Disabilities II, Leadership, and Supervision and Ethics. During that time, I discovered things like: adjustment disorders, anxiety disorders, delirium, dementia, amnestic and other cognitive disorders, dissociative disorders, eating disorders, factitious disorders, impulse-control disorders, mental disorders due to a general medical condition, mood disorders, personality disorders, schizophrenia and other psychotic disorders, sexual and gender identity disorders, sleep disorders, somatoform disorders, and substance-related disorders. This list could go on ad infinitum.

So, I completed the psychiatric technician program and was ready to apply for my licensure from the state. I had to take into consideration that I was an ex-felon at this time because of the wreckage of my past, but I had also discovered a new-found faith in a God that I had established a conscious contact with. I was taught that all I had to do was to put in the footwork and leave the results up to God. So, I applied for my licensure and was allowed to take the test. I passed and received my first state license. I was officially a Licensed Psychiatric Technician (LPT) and proud of it. My level of confidence was off the charts, and I was on a roll.

But it was too early to spike the football, and no victory dance was allowed. During this time, I had moved out of the treatment center, been married and divorced, and lived in pretty much an empty house. Berta and her husband Albert took care of the house, and all I wanted to do was study. I think that this was the time that I became a workaholic (or addicted to school, whichever the term may be), but I never got a hangover from it. I had just started working at West Anaheim TRC part-time, Anaheim General Hospital part-time, and at Fairview Developmental Center full time.

I got a small dining table with chairs somewhere (probably a yard sell), and that became my desk. At this point in my journey, I created my first study zone. This is a place where I listen to classical music, light up some scented candles, and focus on the books. This helps calm my busy mind when things interrupt my tasks at hand, which was now studying.

To earn an Associate Degree, all I needed to do at this point was to complete 25 units of General Education Graduation requirements. So, I took those classes and passed, and that allowed me to get two degrees at once. I took my general education classes and made them my major, with my psychiatric technician classes as my minor, and received my Associates in Arts degree. Then I took my psychiatric technician classes as my major, made my general education classes as my minor, and received my Associates in Science degree.

Since I had made it thus far, I thought that I should move forward, so I transferred over to another community college and entered a transition course. As a licensed psychiatric technician, I qualified for a portion of the registered nursing program that allowed me to bypass the first semester. So, I applied and got accepted into the program.

More and More Education

The registered nursing program is strict, and getting into this program with a history such as mine would be a challenge. What I wanted to know was that if I completed the program, would they allow me to get a license to practice. I contacted the board that monitors people with a troubled history, and they told me that they could not give me an answer until I completed the program and graduated. What if I spent all this time and money to complete this program, and they didn't give me a license? But my faith overcame my fear, and I entered the nursing program. Somewhere in my prayers, God directed me to leave Anaheim General, because I needed more time to focus on the task at hand--mainly, the nursing program. Plus, He had given me Berta, and I think that was His purpose after all.

In transition, I took Introduction to Pharmacology, which focused on the topics of pharmacokinetics and pharmacodynamics. I thought it was interesting to know how drugs work. I smile because I thought that I knew a thing or two about drugs, but this course really expanded my horizon. The new drugs that entered my life were completely different from the ones I had been familiar with.

I started understanding how antimanics like Lithium Carbonate, Carbamazepine, and Lamotrigine worked on enhancing reuptake of amines in the brain. I learned how anti-anxiety medications like Alprazolam, Diazepam, and Lorazepam interact with neurotransmitters to depress the central nervous system. I discovered how there were older and newer antipsychotics like Risperidone, Olanzapine, Quetiapine, Haloperidol, and Chlorpromazine, and the way they act by blocking dopamine receptors throughout the brain to treat psychotic disorders, severe behavior problems in children, and severe nausea, vomiting, and intractable hiccups. This is just a small portion of what I discovered there. But I did study hard, passed the class, and moved forward.

Second semester of nursing was comprised of the nursing process of women, parents, and children of diverse cultures with biological and psychosocial system needs. It focused on growth and development across the life phases, with emphasis on family centered care. In this class I got introduced to labor and delivery.

I have no children and have never seen the birth process before. But now I was learning things like the three stages of labor and terms like lightening, when the decent of the fetal head enters the pelvis. I learned when the mucus plug is expelled, the baby is on its way, and how the spontaneous rupture of the fetal membranes occurs when a woman's water breaks.

I was learning amazing things and having tremendous experiences as I continued, class after class.

I remember being in the delivery room for three c-sections and one vaginal birth. This was an experience that I can never forget—watching all of these babies take their first breaths. It was awesome! I got to do the **A**ppearance, **P**ulse, **G**rimace, **A**ctivity, and **R**espiration (APGAR) test on the new-borns, as well as give them their first injection of vitamin K into their tiny little thigh shortly after birth.

As the semester moved forward, I studied the growth and development of children and the disease process. I cared for children that had cancer, severe burns, surgeries, etc. I then moved into the psych portion of my education. This was familiar, because I had already done the psych tech program, and the information was basically the same.

Third semester of this program was primarily practicing acute concepts, including: fluid and electrolyte balance, metabolism, central nervous system, cellular regulation, oxygenation, perfusion, reproduction, inflammation, infection, mobility, comfort, stress and coping, mood and affect, cognition, safety and infection control, communication, professional behavior, clinical reasoning/judgement, and ethics.

Graduating

By the time that the fourth semester came, I had performed well in my classes and had the confidence of my instructors. We were entering the preceptor portion of our classes, which meant I was ready to develop leadership skills, including time management, prioritization, and delegation in an independent clinical environment. I got the privilege of being assigned in the emergency room at a well-known teaching hospital. Dealing with emergencies all the time was exciting and fast paced. I got to assist in everything from cold symptoms to gunshot wounds to the head.

I was finally done with the nursing program and graduated with my class. We had a nice pinning ceremony,

Education is the Key

and we all went on our way to pursue our careers. I watched many of my classmates get their letters stating that they could take the board test to get their license, but my case took a different turn. Because of the wreckage of my past, the state board informed me that I had a problem with my history and that I couldn't take my test. For a moment, I was hurt. I had worked hard and passed, even surpassed some members of my class. I watched them get jobs as registered nurses and move forward, and here I was, not even allowed to take the test.

I remembered that God had not brought me this far to just leave me now, so I prayed for the knowledge of His will and the power to carry it out. I then took the action that I felt was needed. I had been eleven years sober at this time, and very active in the recovery community. I reached out to all of the people in my support system, and they reminded me of a statement that still rings true: "If you want what we have to offer and are willing to go to any lengths to get it, then you are ready to take certain steps." I wanted what the nursing board had, which was a license, and I was willing to go to any length to get it, so I asked them what was needed for me to do.

Going to Any Lengths

I was informed that the burden of proof lies within me to show them that I have changed. Lucky for me, I have already been down this road before. I put together a 400 page package (including my Certificate of Rehabilitation), detailing everything that I had done over the past nine years that showed the positive progress of my life as it was. I got seventy character reference letters, stating that I have good moral standing. I turned in several years of my work evaluations that were positive. I showed them a track record of my financial growth from the past ten years. I explained in detail all the accounts of my criminal past and explained how my disease of addiction has been arrested, and that I am living a life of recovery. I did all of this and prayed everyday as I have done and still do for the past eighteen years.

While I was waiting for the board to make a decision, I decided to take courses to supplement my time. I had enough college units to get me into a lot of things. With a couple of classes here and there, plus a lot of work experience, I was able to complete a program for addiction study and, because of my recent CAS that I had obtained from Cornerstone, I was able to move up a level in substance treatment and became a Certified Addiction Treatment Counselor (CATC). Then I took a course and became a Certified Anger Management Facilitator (CAMF).

I know that God is still in the miracle business, because less than a year later, I received a letter stating that I was allowed to take the test. If I passed, they would issue me a license but revoke it and reinstate it under a probationary period of three years. Again, God gave me a chance, but I must do the work. I agreed, passed the test, and received my license under probation.

End of My Pursuit

The irony of all this was that my terms of probation were that I would have to go to recovery meetings and do random drug tests. By this time of my life, I had been going to recovery meetings for twelve years, so meetings were part of my life! As far as random drug tests, that was easy too. I haven't taken a drink or a drug for the past 12 years. As far as probation? Well, that was something I had experienced before as well. Also, I had to be supervised by another registered nurse and, because I worked at Fairview, I was able to have the RN there mentor me, and that satisfied my supervision portion. I breezed through that period and was able to get my license restored within three years. I was now an official Registered Nurse (RN).

I figured that I was on a roll and decided to go to a university to get my bachelor's degree. I was told that because I had a past history, I may not get accepted into a school of higher learning. At this time, Fairview was mandating staff to stay over, so they could no longer support my educational goals. The hospital was to be my priority, which was fair, because this is where I was employed full time. But I also had discovered that I have a God that is still in the miracle business, and as long as I remained open, honest, and willing, He would have my back. So, I prayed about it, resigned from Fairview, took on full time work at West Anaheim TRC, applied to the university, told them the truth, and I was accepted. I then applied for employment at Cypress College to be an adjunct instructor and got hired.

When I completed my studies two years later, I received my Bachelor's in Science in Nursing (BSN). After I graduated, I applied and received my Public Health Nurse (PHN) license as well.

In the end of my pursuit of education, I can proudly say that if I wished, I can legally display these initials behind my name: LPT, RN, BSN, PHN, CATC III N, and CAMF. Come to think of it, I have more initials behind my name than I do in my name. Another thing that I've come to realize is that I have been employed and not missed work since 2001. Each job is better than the one previous, and this is why I feel that education is the key! Not bad for an eighth grade drop out.

My education and skills allow me to be able to sit here and write this book. I can say that I am well employed and properly equipped to do many things now. I am a business owner, an educator, and now an author. I have created many programs, which can help those who have had the same problem as I. I do lectures, workshops, classes, and community service.

I want to be the light of encouragement for those who want to go to school but need some motivation to do so. There is so much empowerment in education. I find, personally, the confidence and self-esteem that it has given me is remarkable, and I want to share the wealth to all who will listen. It is possible, and as you can see, it is doable. I believe that everyone can have a chance in life such as I have been given. If I were to ask, 'Why am I here?' now, I would have to say, 'To mention that there's a support network in Southern California that I just learned about at Cypress College campus, that helps provide students with a way up and out. It's called the F.I.T.E. Club (From Incarcerated to Empowered), and I think it is worth checking out.'

Chapter Eleven
Spiritual Awakening

Then there's God….

How do I write about God? I thought about this for a while and have prayed long and often about how to talk about this topic. The result was to just say what's on my mind. This is how I get most of my answers.

I have always believed that there was a God and that He has been in my life forever. However, the God that I knew before my life changed was a God that was in the rescue business. He was a God of Emergency. What I mean by this is that whenever I found myself in serious trouble, I would cry out for Him to help me get out of a situation, because I was either afraid, in pain, or just thoroughly confused. I refer to God as 'Him' because that is what I have been calling Him all of my life. But is God really a Him? Is

God an open space in time that engulfs us all—a forever permeation of existence that is indescribable? Is God a thought in my head, just like the thought that I am receiving now? Forever changing, always expanding, and sometimes fading off into the twilight of my dream? Or is God just a dream waiting for me to wake up to remind me that I have always been dreaming?

There are two things that I have always pondered the secrets of—one is life, and the other is God. There are many books that can give insight into these questions, and I have read several of them. I have prayed, cried out, discussed, argued, and asked about God, and in the end, I have come to my own conclusion.

Seeing God's Hand

I remember in times of need, I begged God for help, and here I am today. Once when I was drinking with friends, our car went over a hill. I prayed and found that a thin little tree held us from going completely over the cliff. Another time, a guy pulled a gun on me and I prayed—he squeezed the trigger anyway. Nothing happened, and I am still here. I remember doing too much heroin, overdosing, and blacking out—yet I am still here. I recall taking so much methamphetamine, my heart beating so fast and forceful, that I thought it was going to rupture a blood vessel, and still, I am here. And when I rode on the back of that moving vehicle, fell off and lost consciousness, aspirating an orange—yet I am still here. I have been through riots where

Spiritual Awakening

people were stabbed, and still, I am here. Even on the day I was born, when the umbilical cord was wrapped around my neck, choking out my very breathe, turning me blue, His hand was on me, and I am still here.

I could go on ad infinitum about how God has saved me from the depths of doom, but is that what God is all about? A God that is only needed when life is unbearable? I can agree with that, because from my experience, God does arrive at those times and far beyond, in my opinion. So, having all of this curiosity, one day I figured that if I want the answer to a question, then the best source should be direct. Many years ago, I got down on my knees and in complete sincerity made this statement to my Higher Power. I said, "God, I know that cars run on gas, and I know that concrete is solid. So how do I know that there is a God?" That was my direct question.

God responds to each of us in a way that is intimate and personal. This is why I feel that some people can only partially understand you when you try to describe what your interpretation of a relationship with God is like or what miracles are to you. What God does for me, how God reveals Himself to me, and what my experience is, is designed for me and me only. This is the only way that I could receive His message in a way that reinforces my beliefs. Some may say that I could be delusional, hallucinating to a certain degree, but that's okay. I work in a psychiatric facility, and I have seen many experiences removed through a variety of medications.

When I asked God that question some sixteen years ago, I was at a park, sober for several years, and rediscovering life on my terms. I was lying on a picnic table and looking into the sky. At that moment, I saw the leaves of the tree above me appear in a three-dimensional view. I drifted into a trance, and when I came out of it, I noticed that there were several species of small wildlife around me. I had an awesome sense of comfort that surrounded me, and to this day, I still feel at peace with myself.

God Shots

Finding God is an interesting concept, because He is never lost. I was lost and had to discover a way to realize that He was still there. I know that some may be uncomfortable with the mention of God and might even wince at the mere hint that something they have never seen might actually exist. I don't feel that there's a monopoly on God and that His omnipotence is felt in one certain way. I once read that Moses experienced a burning bush. I once talked to a bush, but it was a drug induced experience (and no, I'm not insinuating that Moses was on drugs, but he did have a God experience as did Job from the Old Testament.) I know of and have read a variety of spiritual experiences, and have lived through some close encounters of the blessed kind myself.

I have what I call 'God shots,' in which He allows me to feel His presence in my life. After all, look at what He allowed me to experience as I've written about here. I do believe that nothing happens in God's world by mistake, and in my opinion, God is everything. I do know that my job is to openly ask for the knowledge to carry out His will for me on a daily basis and to practice ways to understand what He wants me to do.

At one point I was afraid of getting close to God. I thought that if I got close to Him, I would die. It used to frighten me to feel His presence, but now, it's reassuring that He is with me at all times. I owe my life to God and the things that I am allowed to experience, and I do pray at least twice a day. I like doing it and it's comfortable. In the morning, I hit my knees before I hit my feet. At this time, I give thanks for being alive. When I have time, I tell Him of how grateful I am to have a roof over my head, to have running water, and electricity. And at night, before I climb into bed, I hit my knees again.

Religion is a roadmap. There are many forms of religion and a variety of religious beliefs. Many follow different paths of various religions, but they always seem to end up at the same place. That place is called spirituality. It's ironic how so many wars were fought over different beliefs, but everyone dies, and one thing is for certain…we are no longer on this plain of existence.

Being Spiritual

Now some may argue that there is reincarnation, which I do believe in. However, as a human being reading this book, thinking these current thoughts, breathing in through lungs, using the intercostal muscles and diaphragm to expand the chest cavity to allow air in, we only get this one bite of the apple. I personally do not think that this is my first rodeo as a human, but I also believe that this is my first and only time as being in this particular body. Perhaps one day I'll get the opportunity to pick up this book in some existence, have déjà vu, and possess the skills to articulate who I am to a mass quantity of people and become some groovy scientific discovery. But until then, I'll just stick with my everyday garden verity of spiritual awakening. Now what does that mean to me?

Being spiritual has its ups and downs. There is a price that is paid for this gift I get. It is important for me that I do not put too much emphasis on the things that God allows me to use while I am here on this earth. After all, everything that I have and get to experience is on loan from God anyway. I can truthfully say that I didn't request birth, and I sure didn't come into this existence with the cars, house, education, addiction, jobs, and feelings, and when I die, none of it goes with me. All of it stays here. So, in that sense, all of this is a loan. None of it belongs to me, therefore I cannot rightfully claim to possess it. I can use it all I want as long as I am here, but in the end, it all stays when I'm gone.

It is important for me that I am kind, considerate of others, and look at their needs before my own. This can be tough because some people are mean. Not that they mean to be. It's just something that they have learned throughout the years for various reasons. Some do this to their own detriment, but regardless of what they do or think, I have to respond in kindness.

I know that at one point in time, I was given a supervisor position and sent to be the new boss at a company. In the beginning, all went well because all I did was just observe and watch how others worked. Then about the third month in, I started implementing change, and the majority of the current workers did not appreciate me doing that. The things that were done to me both behind my back as well as to my face were not nice. Some of it actually hurt my feelings, but being the supervisor, I sucked it up. Now what I would have liked to have done was to terminate those who really weren't doing their job, and some did get fired, but I had to pray about each decision to make, being sure that what I was doing what was right and not done out of resentment from how I was treated. I even cried over a few because I knew that some only acted on what they were taught. However, I did have a job to do.

So, what do I get for this price I pay for spirituality? I get comfort and peace of mind. I get to be okay with me in my moments, and when moments are put together, they eventually add up to a lifetime. Being at peace with oneself is the greatest gift that I have found on this plain of existence. I like the fact that my problems don't last long, because I realize that everything that happens is all part of God's plan. Births, deaths, celebrations, accidents, marriages, divorces, money, poverty—all of it is His, and I get to understand that fact deep within the depths of my being.

This allows me to accept everything as it is. In turn, I cease fighting everybody and everything. I can admit that I am not perfect at this and God knows, but I constantly strive for progress on a daily basis. For that I am grateful and have achieved an attitude of gratitude. I have learned to accept everything as it should be, thus allowing me to skip gayly down the pathway of prosperity.

Forgiveness is something that I am gifted with as well. I don't hold a grudge, and that is cool. I know that in an earlier chapter I mention that at the age of nine years old, my sisters and I woke up one day and found that my mother had been shot in the head. This had bothered me for years, and I knew in my heart that my step-father was the one who had done it. I remember when I was eighteen years old, I saw him again and wanted to beat the crap out of him but didn't. I carried that burden with me for years up until I learned that forgiveness was the only way to release myself from that pain. Fourteen years ago, I went to his gravesite and asked him to forgive me for all the trouble that I had caused him, and that I was sorry for holding that grudge. I also spoke to his grave and forgave him for all the troubles that I felt that he imposed on me through my youth. That day, I felt such a relief and felt some burden lift from me.

I have learned that when you let things go, God has room to give you more. Believe me, I have way more than I could have asked for. However, letting things go and grasping them back happens all the time. This is why we celebrate the little things and are happy with progress, for it is better than perfection.

Spiritual Awakening

In my life, my adapting to being homeless and accepting that as a lifestyle (including incarceration and drug abuse) only strengthened it, and it became the new norm. I always equate this to having only exercised your right arm. With years of practice, this arm gets stronger and easier to use. It becomes the new norm, regardless of how out of the norm it is. Now as I have started learning how to use my skinny left arm, life is different. Things are new—getting and keeping a job, not drinking or using drugs. Putting others needs before my own was difficult in the beginning. Every time I was expected to use this new arm, there were growing pains. In the beginning, whenever something didn't go right, it was uncomfortable, and the old arm was easier to pull out. But with time, I trained myself to use this new arm and now have grown into living happily in this new life that I was given.

Chapter Twelve
Park Bench

The final chapter of this book is here, and how do I close such an interesting journey? You have walked with me through some incredible times. It's ironic how sixty years of life can be summed up into a minute amount of pages. I smile because literally, you have my life in your hands, and with what you see, it actually can make a difference.

I have spent many years behind some type of wall—physical, emotional, and psychological. Homelessness, abuse, and addiction was a wall to me as well. Here, when I thought that I was trying to protect myself, I ended up being my own jailer. I was a prisoner, locked within myself with no way out. All I could do was to look out at the world and wish that things were different, realizing that it was for everybody else.

As you have read, with years of growth, I can

truthfully say that I have made it beyond my prison and have experienced impossible realities. As you conclude this book, I want you to know that I have reached those dreams. I started off a child full of fear, and now I am an adult full of self confidence and self-esteem. With God's guidance, love, and gentle hands, I was able to work my way up from a park bench to becoming a respected member of society. I was guided to come out and let people see that no matter how far down in life you can get, there is still a way up and out; I hope that my experience will be able to benefit others. Furthermore, I am driven by what I see every day—whether it's on the news or in my face—and I feel the need to do something that is greater than myself. Having found joy, peace, comfort, and happiness, with a clear mind, I do feel a new freedom. Now it's time to carry a message of hope, faith, and love.

As I have said in the beginning, one of the purposes of this book is to create funding for the house that you see on the back cover. To date, as you come to the final pages, there is already a person living in the house and starting to get things off the ground. He was homeless, just as I was, and has issues, just as those that you have read. He is finding his way, and I am grateful to be of service in a way that is allowing the cycle of trauma to be understood and the facilitation of hope to be implemented.

Brown Manor

His name is George, and I must confess, he is my nephew. I was speaking with him recently, and he informed

Park Bench

me of the fact that there may be an issue getting the electricity turned on at Brown Manor. He also stated that the roof is badly in need of repair. He then informed me about the broken windows, the walls that needed to be replaced, and the water damage on the ceiling panels. I stayed silent because that's what I do when I ponder serious matters such as this. I know for sure that I don't have that type of cash lying around, but that is why I am writing this book, remember. The proceeds will all go to getting Brown Manor up and sustaining it while it shelters others. The best I could do is turn all of this over to God at this time (as I have been doing for years). I hit my knees and asked for God's guidance and the knowledge of His will for me. George questioned my silence, and he asked me a question that must've been on his mind. He asked, "Uncle, why did you buy this place?"

    At this time, I felt the need to share this thought with him, for this was the first time that I told him of the big picture, of what this is all for. I told him that I knew a person who was homeless, strung out on drugs, and didn't know how to ask for help. I let him know that this person was lost and lived in temporary shelters, but could never stay in one place long enough to call home because of the issues that he had to deal with. I told him that over time, this person got tired of trying when there seems to be no break in sight and that when all hope was lost, he stopped feeling like a human being. During my conversation with George, I also revealed how difficult it was when all you have is poor choices, which is what led this person to make poor decisions. I shared how a person could find incarceration as the only way to get rest and that this person was caught in a forever cycle that leads to homelessness and eventually hopelessness.

I told him that he was part of something bigger than him and me. I told him that he is helping to create a community that can assist those who need a break but cannot find one. This is important because it is an example of what a person can do when receiving positive support for doing positive things, but first needs a positive place to learn how to make positive decisions. I informed him that by sweeping the floors, he is being of service to clean his house, subsequently setting a foundation of something far greater than what mere words could say. He was giving to the Universe, and in return, the Universe will bless him in abundance. Honest hard work does pay off, and everything happens in God's time, not ours. I shared with him how I feel the presence of God, and every chance I get, I stop and listen for His voice. I informed him that I was led to do this project, and all I know right now is that if I do the foot work and leave the results up to God, the results are always the way that He wants us to have them. Our job is to ask Him for the power to carry out His will and the insight into what that is.

George stayed quiet throughout my pitch. When I was done, he simply replied, "Okay Unk".

I wonder if this is what Noah felt when he was instructed to build the ark. Noah was 600 years old when God told him to start that construction, and according to Genesis, it took him 120 years to complete that project.

So, I guess I still have a few years to get this house up and running. I smile, because by the mere fact that you are reading this book, you are all a part of the story of Brown Manor.

I exposed myself in this book to demonstrate and educate those out there that we, as human beings, all have our problems. There are skeletons in every human's closet. Everyone has them in some way, shape, or form. Admitting them to others is challenging at best. Being homeless, addicted, and slightly psychotic up until 1999 was a tough pill to swallow when it comes to my reality. Facing childhood abuse was another, but I made it and was allowed the gift of sharing my travels with you. I want those who are afraid to look inward to understand that there is a reason why the world that we live in is a by-product of what we have allowed ourselves to create. Pain is a touchstone to growth, however, suffering is optional.

We still have a long way to go when it comes to dealing with illnesses, whether its addiction or mental illness. I hope that being aware of what it's like to live in those shoes can illuminate some of the darkness that stigmas have placed on this population. I have gone literally from a Park Bench to a very good life to which I refer as Park Avenue. I have an ease of mind and sense of accomplishment in my life because of this journey. I have a career, an education, a home, vehicles, and a belief in God that is so strong that it illuminates in my everyday living. I live in the sunlight of The Spirit.

I do find myself mediating at the park on occasions, while remembering where I came from. This I should never forget. These days, instead of being full of fear and anxiety, I notice the simple things in life like: ducks, waterfalls, and people, all the while realizing that within me is a state of calmness that I wish I could just cast out into the wind so that everyone may enjoy a moment of tranquility. While hanging out on a park bench, I continue to meditate on the blessings and wonders of life. The musings are amusing to say the least, for there is still a lot of work to do.

Don't Stop, Keep Going

A friend of mine (who is currently drinking and using drugs) called me up and needed a ride home from work. I said okay and picked her up. She was displaying involuntary muscle movements (twitching) and reeked of alcohol. She was rehashing the same thing about how messed up her roommates are, how she hated her job, her life, and the world around her. She stated that she is someday going to get better. This person has lost her car, lost her license, has little education, and rents a room where doing drugs and constant conflict is the norm. On the way to her home, we saw a homeless lady with a sign out. I was going to stop to give this lady some change, but my friend started to get agitated saying, "No, don't stop, keep going." Then she went on to tell me why I shouldn't help someone out because of the situation that they are in and that they should get their life together. This is what it is. Denial is a tough nut to crack.

Park Bench

There is a drug epidemic going on out there, and something must be done about it. We seemed baffled with finding a way to face and find solutions to the issue of homelessness. Mental illness is everywhere, and I see these problems affecting all walks of life—from the poor and homeless to the rich and famous. I have seen addiction from both ends of the spectrum and want to be part of the needed change. No, I cannot say I want to do something; by writing this book, I AM doing something.

My contribution to this crisis is to show you that there is a solution. I have lived through trauma and discovered resiliency. I have lived through addiction and found recovery. I have been incarcerated and discovered rehabilitation. I have been homeless and found residency. All of these are facts, and the bottom line is that we all have our story. A story which is no different than what you have read. A story in which the truth has made me experience a freedom from self, and only when we feel free, we can heal unconditionally. Empathy, by the way, is different than sympathy.

Always remember that when you drive down the street and see a homeless person, or walk past a pile of things that seem to be abandoned garbage, just think that this individual is a person, is another me. When you enter a hospital for care or are sitting in a classroom taking notes from a professor, just think that this individual is another me. When you see someone talking to themselves or attending a church service praising God, that person is me.

Thank you for allowing me to grow through this story. Writing this book has given me more than what I could have imagined. I got to review some harsh truths, shed some much-needed tears, and laughed at my own insanity. I have felt a renewed sense of gratitude, not just for myself, but for those around me. I am truly grateful today. "Grateful people are happy people and those that aren't, aren't. "

I metaphorically live on a pink cloud every day, almost every minute that I am awake.

Life today, at this very moment, is groovy.

Always remember this simple sentence:

One Light Does Make a Difference.

Acknowledgements

I have to give thanks to some of the people who have made the contents of this book possible. I have to thank Jeannette B. for giving me the ability to experience this thing called life. She was my mother and her strength and perseverance through life has inspired me to believe that I can do anything if I put my mind to it. Even though she has never told me those words directly, her actions towards this spoke volumes.

I have to thank Patricia B., who for over 20 years has nurtured me, put up with me and pushed my fingers to the keyboard. I met her within a virtual world called, "A Creek," in an AOL chatroom. Even though I have never physically met this woman, she has inspired me on numerous occasions to believe in myself. She loved me until I finally learned how to love myself.

I have to give thanks to Nancy C., who saw a light in me that I never knew could be lit. She saw something in me that was hidden and brought it out for the world to see. She was the first person who introduced me to the path that I call home, a new life that I never knew existed and was afraid to encounter.

I have to give thanks to Cindy W and Maurice K., whose expensive boot guided me into taking this step. They volunteered their time to teach me financial sensibility to the point where it hurt. They continue to be a big part of my life, in spite of my fears of the world when it comes to fiscal responsibility.

I have to thank Debbie M., who always believed in me, and for our late-night conversations that we share and the support that she provides when it comes to teaching me how to be a respectable person in this world. She teaches me what "a mother's love" and family is all about.

I have to give thanks to Sherry at Square Tree Publishing for guiding me through the aspects of how to be a writer. When she asked me in the beginning if she could pray for me, I knew that God had His hands in this. I also must recognize Melodie for her patience with me throughout the editing process.

I have to thank God for His omnipotence and omnipresence in my life. Without His hand, I would not have made this journey.

And most important Sparrow / Woodstock, whose tears are the water to my soul.

Support Brown Manor
The Home for the Homeless

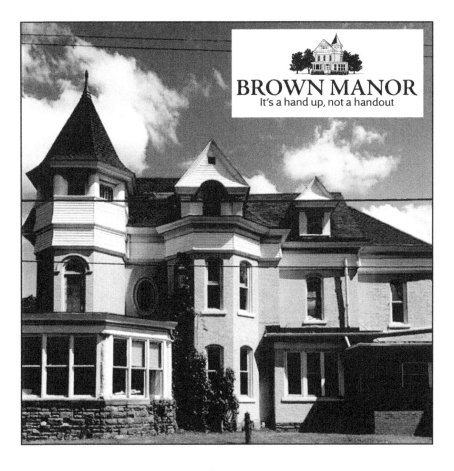

Go to:

anthonyhowardbrown.com/brownmanor

Guest Speaker

Anthony Brown
www.anthonyhowardbrown.com

Author, Speaker, Professor

Anthony Brown is the founder and director of Coordinating & Assisting Recovery Environments (C.A.R.E.), located in Anaheim, California. Since 1999, Anthony's passion is providing specialized treatment for individuals who suffer with mental illness combined with a substance use disorder. With a B.S. in Nursing from California State University Fullerton, Anthony developed and directed a long-term residential treatment model, which has fueled his dream to open a home for those who have suffered from the disease of addiction and mental illness. Knowing firsthand what homelessness and addiction are like, Anthony's amazing story provides hope and help on the journey to wholeness and recovery.

Topics:
- How to Effectively Help the Homeless
- Overcoming Childhood Trauma
- Overcoming Obstacles and Pushing Through Adversity

Event Venues:
- Conferences
- Church Services
- Seminars
- Schools
- Key Note

Book to Speak
Email: info@anthonyhowardbrown.com

At **SQUARE TREE PUBLISHING**, we believe your message matters. That is why our dedicated team of professionals is committed to bringing your literary texts and targeted curriculum to a global marketplace. We strive to make that message of the highest quality, while still maintaining your voice. We believe in you, therefore, we provide a platform through website design, blogs, and social media campaigns to showcase your unique message. Our innovative team offers a full range of services from editing to graphic design inspired with an eye for excellence, so that your message is clearly and distinctly heard.

Whether you are a new writer needing guidance with each step of the process, or a seasoned writer, we will propel you to the next level of your development.

At **SQUARE TREE PUBLISHING**, it's all about **you**.

Sign up for a free consultation.

Your opportunity is "Write Outside the Box"!

www.SquareTreePublishing.com

Made in the USA
Middletown, DE
01 March 2023